# INVESTMENT STRATEGY BOOK

Loren Lawrence

Copy Right@2021, all right reserved.

# Introduction

This book can help you to plan your investment strategy base on the **Elliott Wave Principle**.

You can check the attractive stock and record the stock price variation and plan your investment strategies.

For example, If the stock on "Rising tendency cycle". You can plan to buy the stock when "Corrective Waves" is finished, which is the location P3 in the figure on "Part One - Rising tendency cycle". You can buy the stock at price P2 when P2 comes again. Then you can sell the stock near the "Golden ratio", which is shown as P4 in the figure. You can pre-calculate the estimated value table of P4 and write on the table. Then you can check and record which price the stock stop and turn direction.

On the contrary, if the stock is on the "Falling tendency cycle ". You can plan to oversell stock when "Corrective Waves" is finished, which is the location P3 in the figure on "Part Two - Falling tendency cycle". You can oversell the stock at price P2 when P2 comes again. Then you can buy the stock back near the "Golden ratio", which is shown as P4 in the figure. You can pre-calculate the estimated value table of P4 and write on the table. Then you can check and record which price the stock stop and turn direction.

**Before you execute the real investment, check record the price variation for a period is essential homework.**
**IF you have no feeling of the stock price variation, do not put your money into the market!**

**Another essential concept is the "Risk-reward ratio" (as RED).**
No one can sure the stock will go up or fall tomorrow.
So you must decide your own **RED** and keep in mind.

**RED** should be 1:2 or 1:3 normally
You choose **RED** as 1:2, this means if you only allow losing one dollar, you should estimate that you could earn two dollars as the target.

Two things you should keep in mind:
(1) If you lose more than one dollar, clean the stock without hesitation! This is the only way to keep your assets!
(2) If you earn more the two dollars, you should sell all the stock.

Remember, you should earn the money by following the strategy you choose!
The market is always right there.
You can make money at any time.
Just follow your correct strategery is enough!

Wish this book can help you earn more money in the market!

# EXAMPLE

# EXAMPLE 1 : Rising Tendency Cycle of APPLE INC.

| Company name: | Apple Inc. |
|---|---|
| stock code: | APPL |

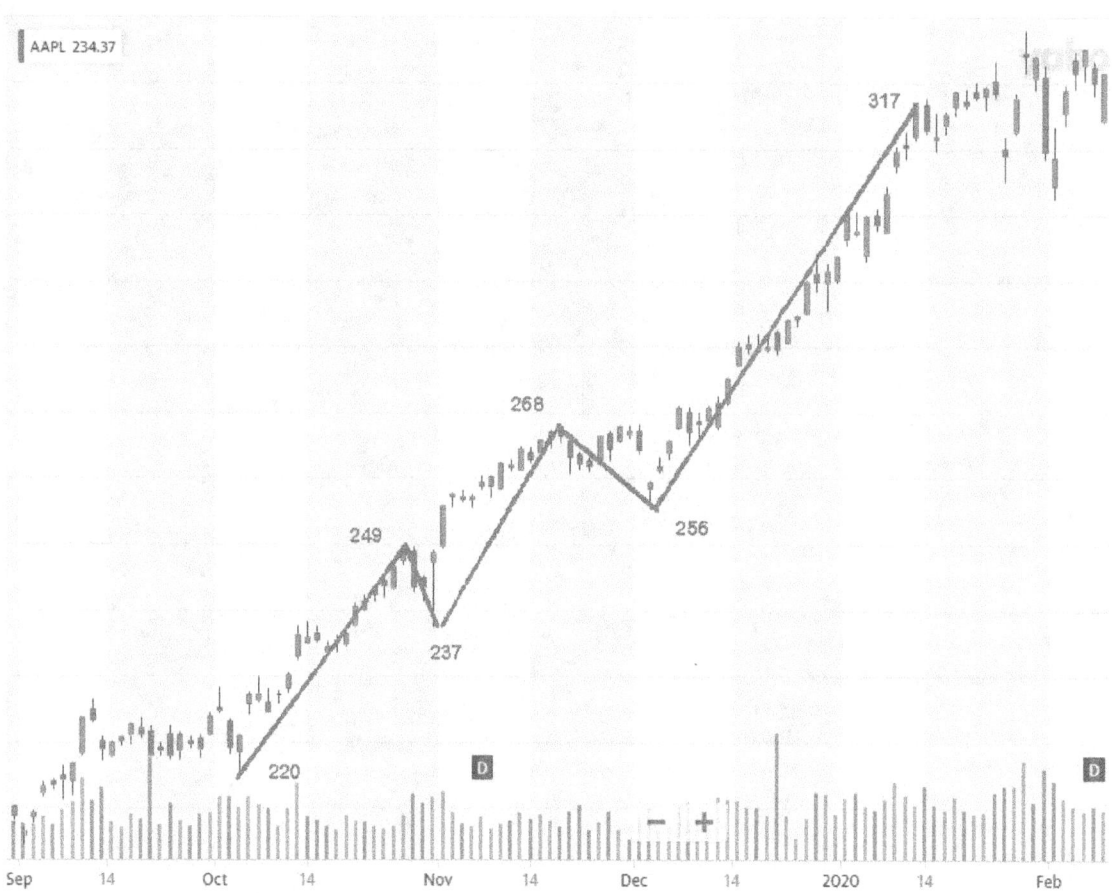

| P4 POSSIBLE VALUE | I=P2-P1 | 249-220=29 |
|---|---|---|
| | P1+I*1.382= | 260.08 |
| | P1+I*1.618= | 266.9 |

| Risk-reward ratio | Estimated Buying price | Estimated Selling price | Acceptable Loss price | Profit (or loss) (according to Risk-reward ratio) |
|---|---|---|---|---|
| 1:2 | 249 | 255 (=249+6) | 246 | 6 [=249-246)*2] |
| 1:3 | 249 | 258 (=249+9) | 246 | 9 [=249-246)*3] |
| 1:2 | 249 | 273 (=249+24) | 237 | 24 [=249-237)*2] |
|  |  |  |  |  |
|  |  |  |  |  |
|  |  |  |  |  |
|  |  |  |  |  |
|  |  |  |  |  |
|  |  |  |  |  |
|  |  |  |  |  |
|  |  |  |  |  |
|  |  |  |  |  |
|  |  |  |  |  |
|  |  |  |  |  |
|  |  |  |  |  |
|  |  |  |  |  |

NOTE: EXAMPLE ONLY

**(1) The profit should be determinate by your loss tolerance!**

(2) The same Risk-reward ratio can be different conclusion.

(3) Normal condition the possible value of P4 is around 1.382 or 1.618. Higher than 1.618 is not normal!

**(4) Never forget the tolerance of risk!**

## EXAMPLE 2 : Falling Tendency Cycle of APPLE INC.

| Company name: | Apple Inc. |
|---|---|
| stock code: | APPL |

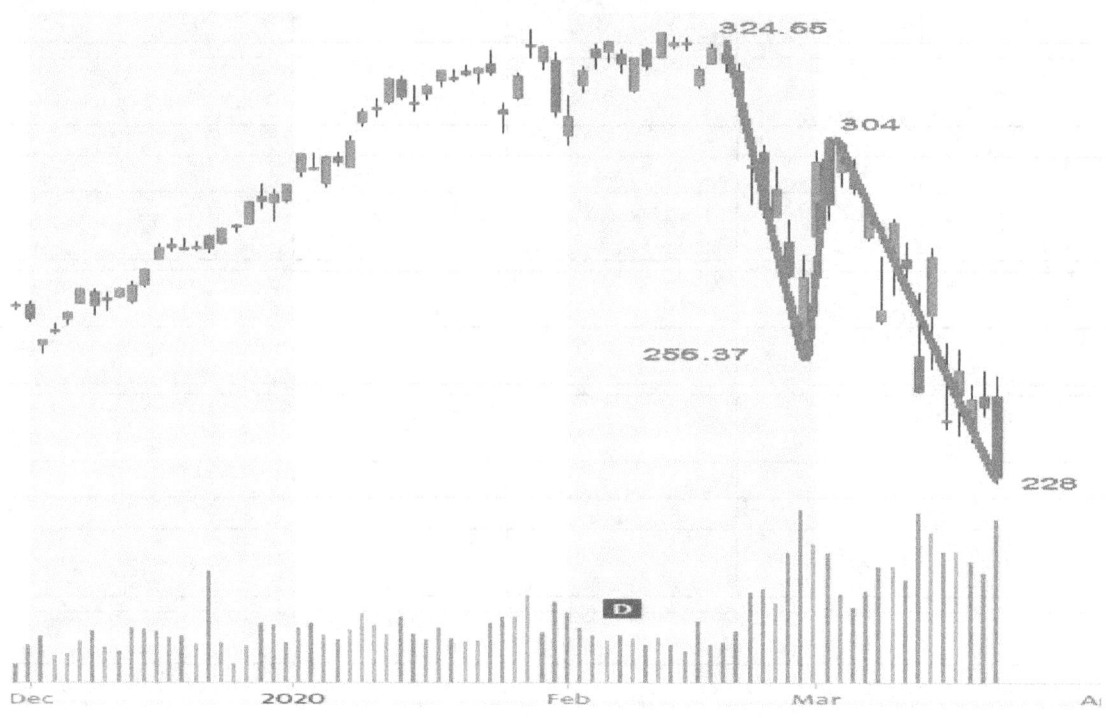

| P4 | I=P1-P2 | 324.65-256.37=68.28 |
|---|---|---|
| POSSIBLE | P1-I*1.382= | 230.28 |
| VALUE | P1-I*1.618= | 214.17 |

| Risk-reward ratio | Estimated Buying back price | Estimated Overselling price | Acceptable Loss price | Profit (or loss) (according to Risk-reward ratio) |
|---|---|---|---|---|
| 1:2 | 248 (=256-8) | 256 | 260 | 8 [=(260-256)*2)] |
| 1:3 | 244 (=256-12) | 256 | 260 | 12 [=(260-256)*2)] |
| 1:2 | 232 (=256-24) | 256 | 268 | 24 [=(260-256)*2)] |
|  |  |  |  |  |
|  |  |  |  |  |
|  |  |  |  |  |
|  |  |  |  |  |
|  |  |  |  |  |
|  |  |  |  |  |
|  |  |  |  |  |
|  |  |  |  |  |
|  |  |  |  |  |
|  |  |  |  |  |
|  |  |  |  |  |
|  |  |  |  |  |
|  |  |  |  |  |

NOTE: EXAMPLE ONLY

**(1) The profit should be determinate by your loss tolerance!**

(2) The same Risk-reward ratio can be different conclusion.

(3) Normal condition the possible value of P4 is around 1.382 or 1.618. Higher than 1.618 is not normal!

**(4) Never forget the tolerance of risk!**

# Part One

## Rising Tendency Cycle

| Company name: | |
|---|---|
| stock code: | |

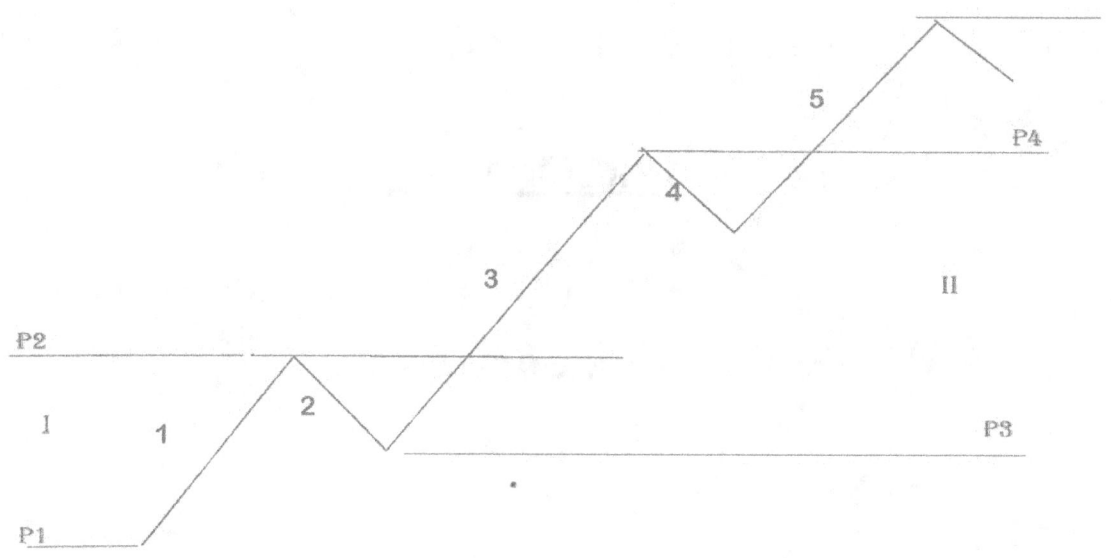

| P4 | I=P2-P1 | |
|---|---|---|
| POSSIBLE | P1+I*1.382= | |
| VALUE | P1+I*1.618= | |

| Risk-reward ratio | Estimated Buying price | Estimated Selling price | Acceptable Loss price | Profit (or loss) (according to Risk-reward ratio) |
|---|---|---|---|---|
| | | | | |
| | | | | |
| | | | | |
| | | | | |
| | | | | |
| | | | | |
| | | | | |
| | | | | |
| | | | | |
| | | | | |
| | | | | |
| | | | | |
| | | | | |
| | | | | |
| | | | | |

NOTE:
_____
_____
_____
_____
_____
_____

| Company name: | |
|---|---|
| stock code: | |

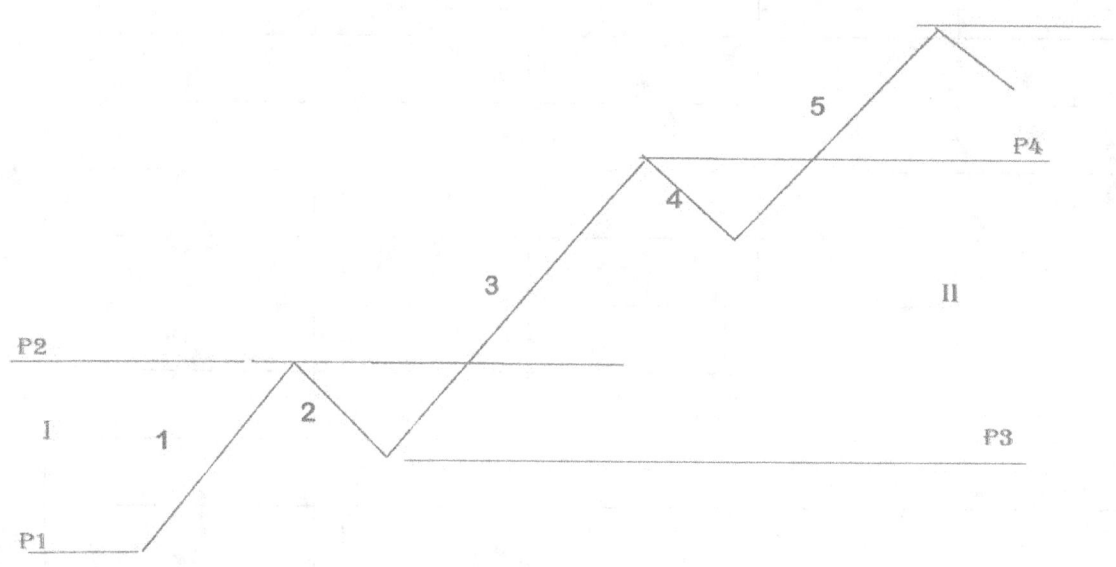

| P4 | I=P2-P1 | |
|---|---|---|
| POSSIBLE | P1+I*1.382= | |
| VALUE | P1+I*1.618= | |

| Risk-reward ratio | Estimated Buying price | Estimated Selling price | Acceptable Loss price | Profit (or loss) (according to Risk-reward ratio) |
|---|---|---|---|---|
| | | | | |
| | | | | |
| | | | | |
| | | | | |
| | | | | |
| | | | | |
| | | | | |
| | | | | |
| | | | | |
| | | | | |
| | | | | |
| | | | | |
| | | | | |
| | | | | |
| | | | | |
| | | | | |
| | | | | |

NOTE:
_____
_____
_____
_____
_____
_____

| Company name: | |
| stock code: | |

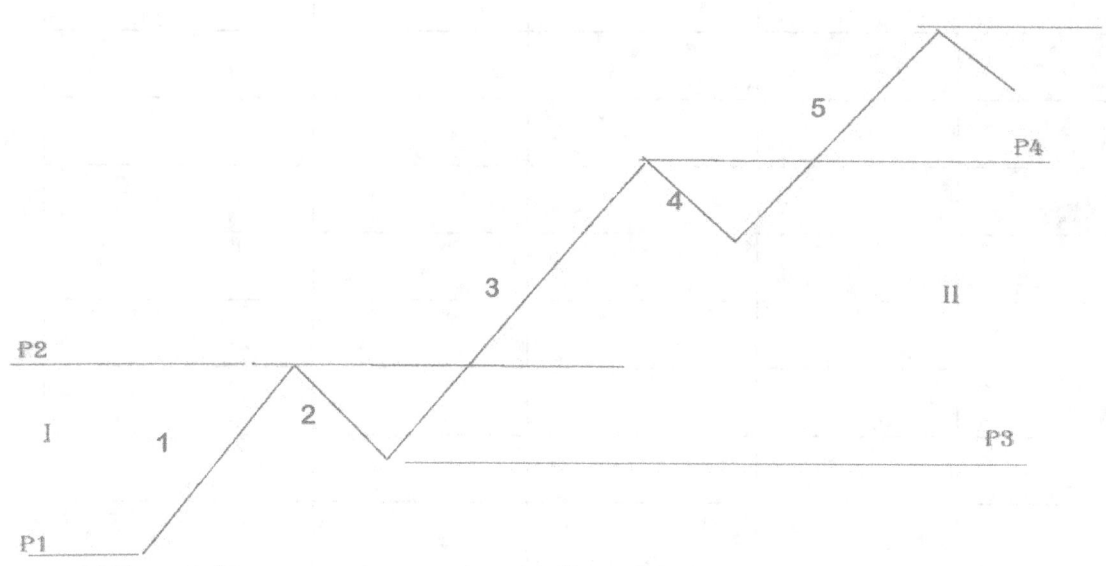

| P4 | I=P2-P1 | |
| --- | --- | --- |
| POSSIBLE | P1+I*1.382= | |
| VALUE | P1+I*1.618= | |

| Risk-reward ratio | Estimated Buying price | Estimated Selling price | Acceptable Loss price | Profit (or loss) (according to Risk-reward ratio) |
|---|---|---|---|---|
| | | | | |
| | | | | |
| | | | | |
| | | | | |
| | | | | |
| | | | | |
| | | | | |
| | | | | |
| | | | | |
| | | | | |
| | | | | |
| | | | | |
| | | | | |
| | | | | |
| | | | | |

NOTE:
_____
_____
_____
_____
_____
_____

| Company name: | |
|---|---|
| stock code: | |

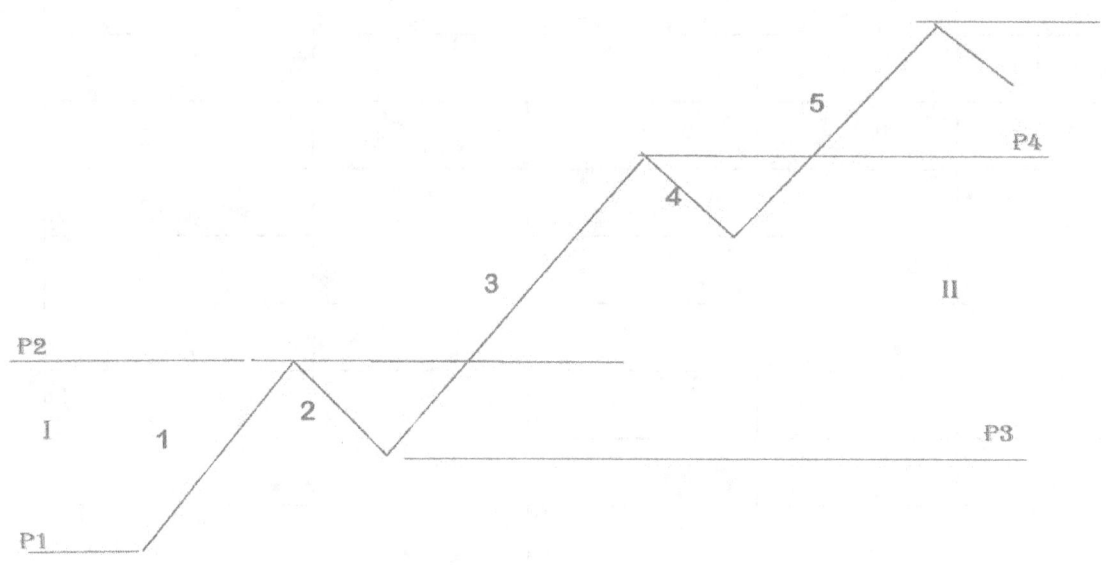

| P4 | I=P2-P1 | |
|---|---|---|
| POSSIBLE | P1+I*1.382= | |
| VALUE | P1+I*1.618= | |

| Risk-reward ratio | Estimated Buying price | Estimated Selling price | Acceptable Loss price | Profit (or loss) (according to Risk-reward ratio) |
|---|---|---|---|---|
| | | | | |
| | | | | |
| | | | | |
| | | | | |
| | | | | |
| | | | | |
| | | | | |
| | | | | |
| | | | | |
| | | | | |
| | | | | |
| | | | | |
| | | | | |
| | | | | |
| | | | | |
| | | | | |

NOTE:
_____
_____
_____
_____
_____
_____

| Company name: | |
|---|---|
| stock code: | |

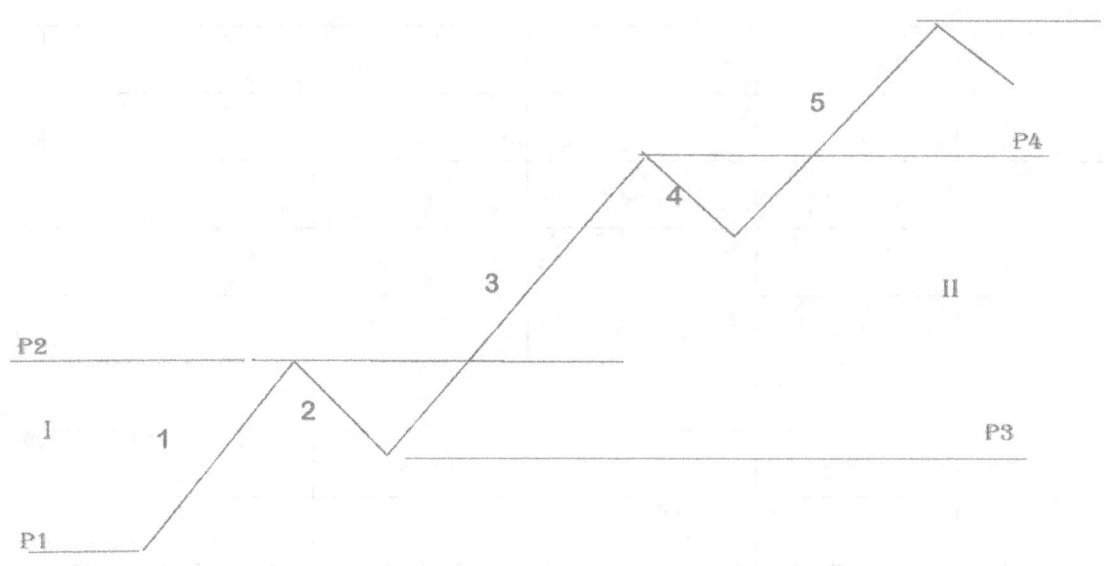

| P4 | I=P2-P1 | |
|---|---|---|
| POSSIBLE | P1+I*1.382= | |
| VALUE | P1+I*1.618= | |

| Risk-reward ratio | Estimated Buying price | Estimated Selling price | Acceptable Loss price | Profit (or loss) (according to Risk-reward ratio) |
|---|---|---|---|---|
| | | | | |
| | | | | |
| | | | | |
| | | | | |
| | | | | |
| | | | | |
| | | | | |
| | | | | |
| | | | | |
| | | | | |
| | | | | |
| | | | | |
| | | | | |
| | | | | |
| | | | | |

NOTE:

| Company name: | |
|---|---|
| stock code: | |

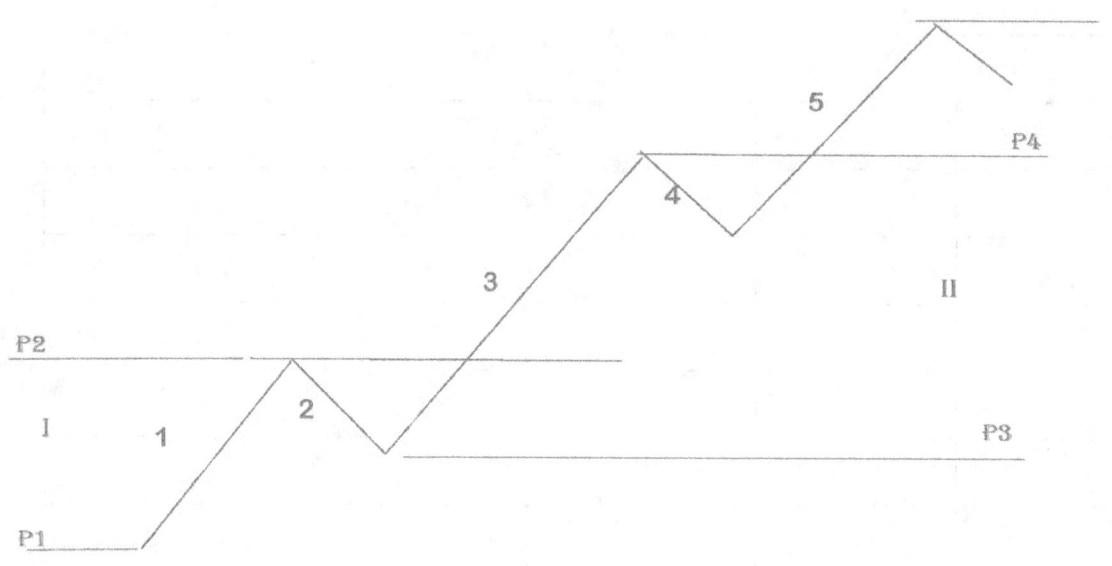

| P4 | I=P2-P1 | |
|---|---|---|
| POSSIBLE | P1+I*1.382= | |
| VALUE | P1+I*1.618= | |

| Risk-reward ratio | Estimated Buying price | Estimated Selling price | Acceptable Loss price | Profit (or loss) (according to Risk-reward ratio) |
|---|---|---|---|---|
| | | | | |
| | | | | |
| | | | | |
| | | | | |
| | | | | |
| | | | | |
| | | | | |
| | | | | |
| | | | | |
| | | | | |
| | | | | |
| | | | | |
| | | | | |
| | | | | |
| | | | | |
| | | | | |

NOTE:
_____
_____
_____
_____
_____
_____
_____

| Company name: | |
|---|---|
| stock code: | |

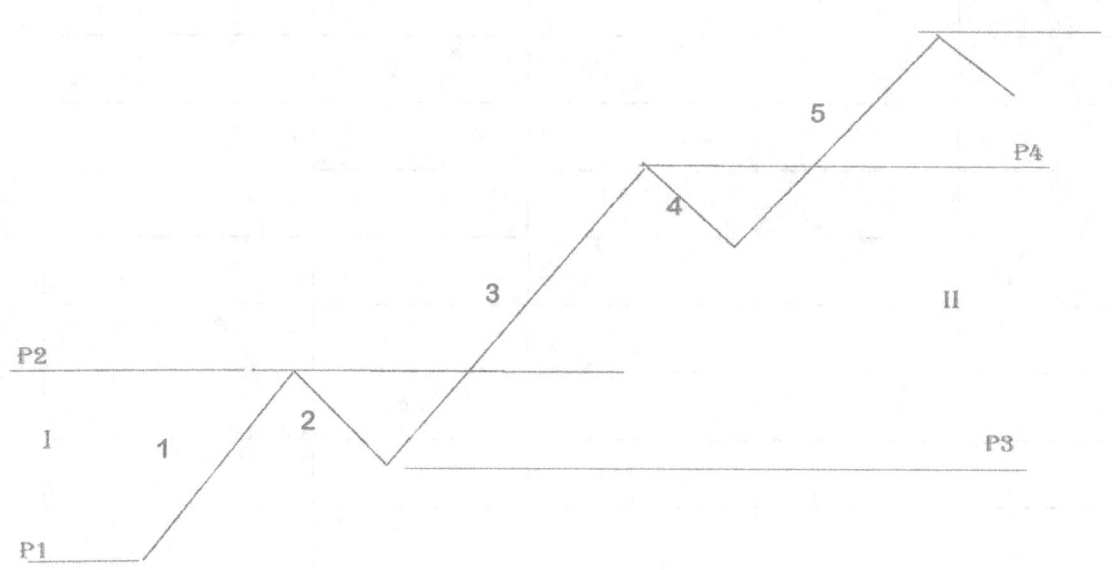

| P4 | I=P2-P1 | |
|---|---|---|
| POSSIBLE | P1+I*1.382= | |
| VALUE | P1+I*1.618= | |

| Risk-reward ratio | Estimated Buying price | Estimated Selling price | Acceptable Loss price | Profit (or loss) (according to Risk-reward ratio) |
|---|---|---|---|---|
| | | | | |
| | | | | |
| | | | | |
| | | | | |
| | | | | |
| | | | | |
| | | | | |
| | | | | |
| | | | | |
| | | | | |
| | | | | |
| | | | | |
| | | | | |
| | | | | |
| | | | | |
| | | | | |

NOTE:

| Company name: | |
|---|---|
| stock code: | |

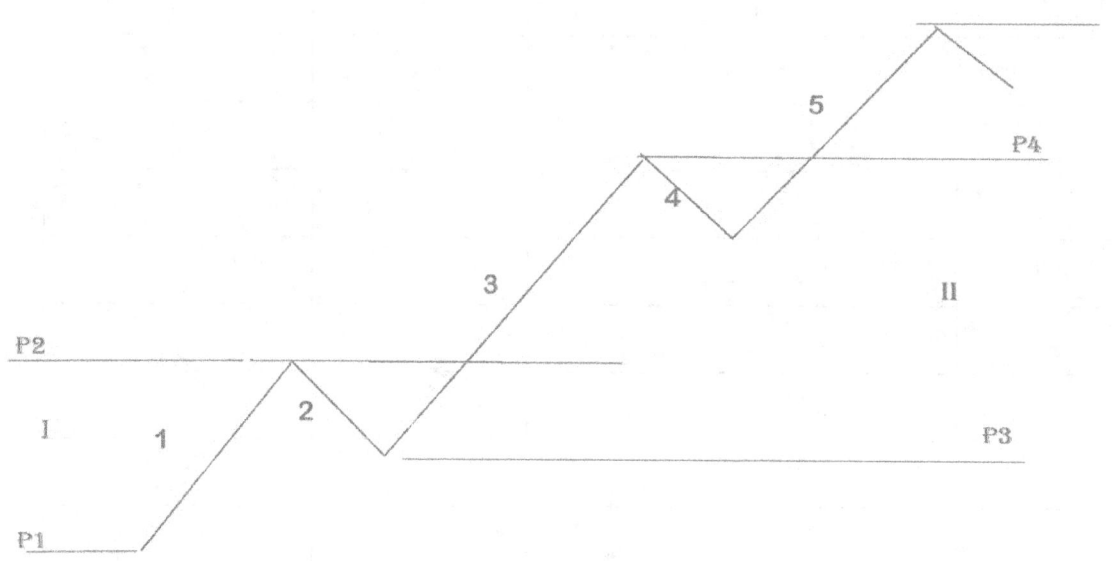

| P4 | I=P2-P1 | |
|---|---|---|
| POSSIBLE | P1+I*1.382= | |
| VALUE | P1+I*1.618= | |

| Risk-reward ratio | Estimated Buying price | Estimated Selling price | Acceptable Loss price | Profit (or loss) (according to Risk-reward ratio) |
|---|---|---|---|---|
| | | | | |
| | | | | |
| | | | | |
| | | | | |
| | | | | |
| | | | | |
| | | | | |
| | | | | |
| | | | | |
| | | | | |
| | | | | |
| | | | | |
| | | | | |
| | | | | |
| | | | | |

NOTE:
_____
_____
_____
_____
_____
_____

| Company name: | |
|---|---|
| stock code: | |

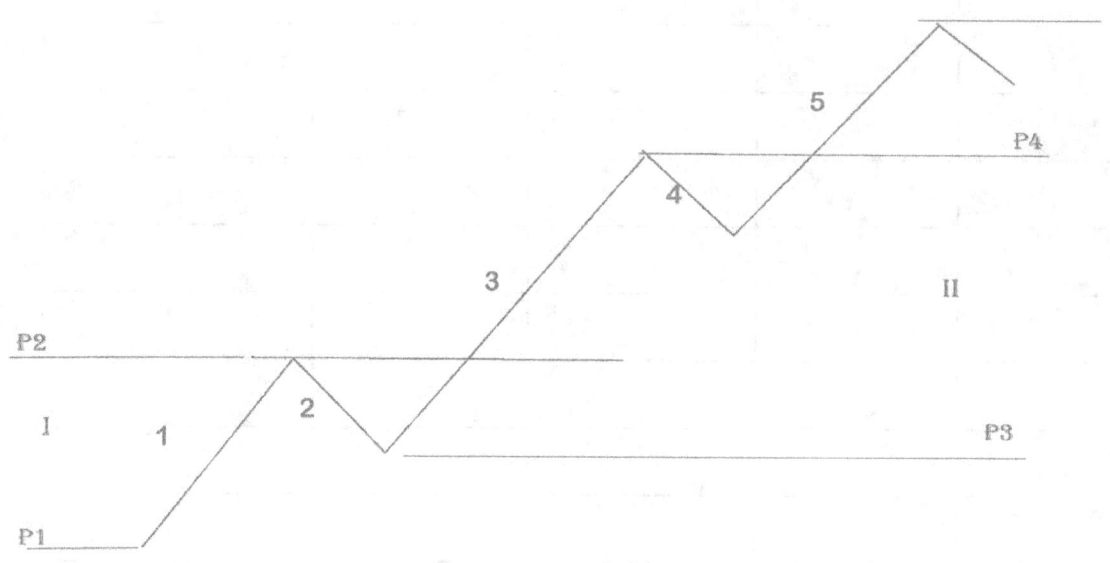

| P4 | I=P2-P1 | |
|---|---|---|
| POSSIBLE | P1+I*1.382= | |
| VALUE | P1+I*1.618= | |

| Risk-reward ratio | Estimated Buying price | Estimated Selling price | Acceptable Loss price | Profit (or loss) (according to Risk-reward ratio) |
|---|---|---|---|---|
| | | | | |
| | | | | |
| | | | | |
| | | | | |
| | | | | |
| | | | | |
| | | | | |
| | | | | |
| | | | | |
| | | | | |
| | | | | |
| | | | | |
| | | | | |
| | | | | |
| | | | | |
| | | | | |

NOTE:

| Company name: | |
|---|---|
| stock code: | |

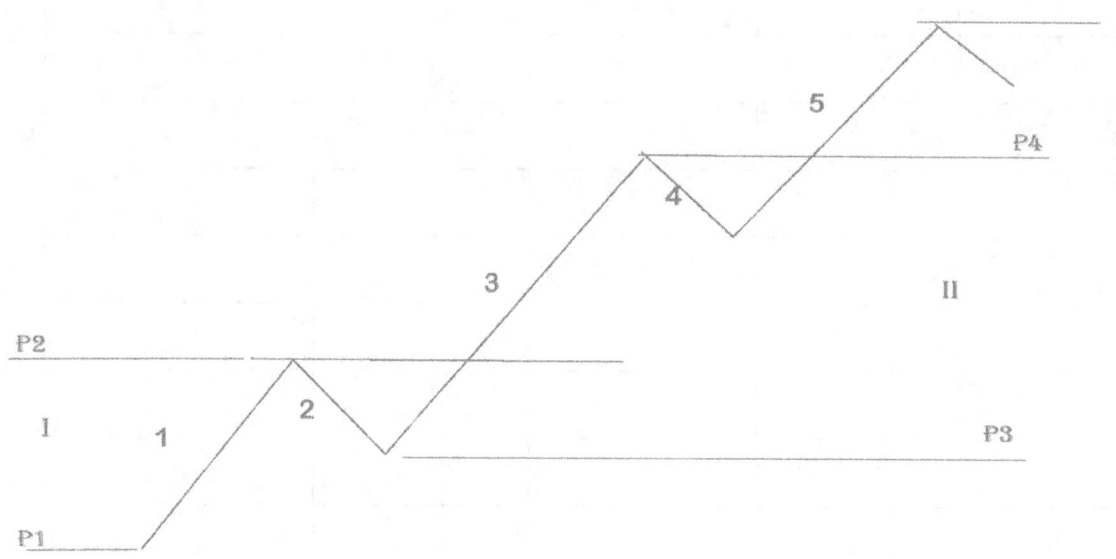

| P4 | I=P2-P1 | |
|---|---|---|
| POSSIBLE | P1+I*1.382= | |
| VALUE | P1+I*1.618= | |

| Risk-reward ratio | Estimated Buying price | Estimated Selling price | Acceptable Loss price | Profit (or loss) (according to Risk-reward ratio) |
|---|---|---|---|---|
| | | | | |
| | | | | |
| | | | | |
| | | | | |
| | | | | |
| | | | | |
| | | | | |
| | | | | |
| | | | | |
| | | | | |
| | | | | |
| | | | | |
| | | | | |
| | | | | |
| | | | | |

NOTE:

| Company name: | |
|---|---|
| stock code: | |

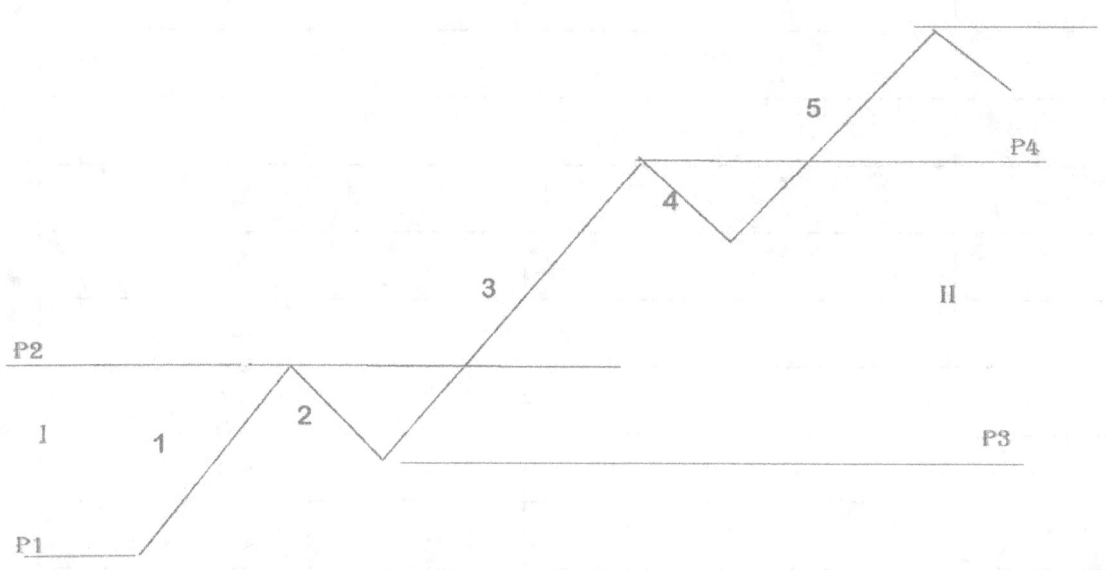

| P4 | I=P2-P1 | |
|---|---|---|
| POSSIBLE | P1+I*1.382= | |
| VALUE | P1+I*1.618= | |

| Risk-reward ratio | Estimated Buying price | Estimated Selling price | Acceptable Loss price | Profit (or loss) (according to Risk-reward ratio) |
|---|---|---|---|---|
| | | | | |
| | | | | |
| | | | | |
| | | | | |
| | | | | |
| | | | | |
| | | | | |
| | | | | |
| | | | | |
| | | | | |
| | | | | |
| | | | | |
| | | | | |
| | | | | |
| | | | | |
| | | | | |

NOTE: _____
_____
_____
_____
_____
_____
_____

| Company name: | |
|---|---|
| stock code: | |

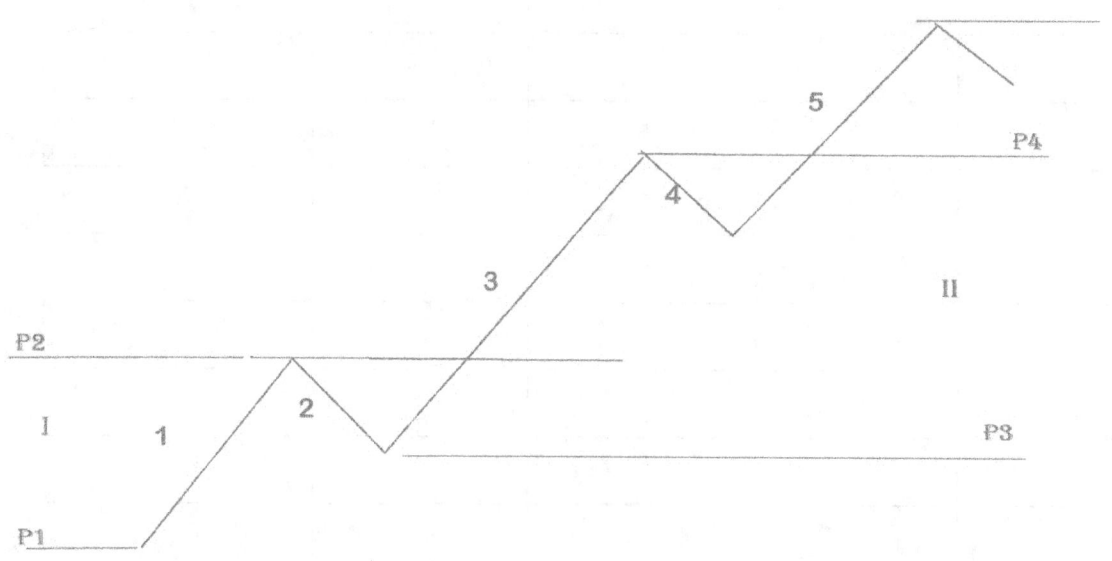

| P4 | I=P2-P1 | |
|---|---|---|
| POSSIBLE | P1+I*1.382= | |
| VALUE | P1+I*1.618= | |

| Risk-reward ratio | Estimated Buying price | Estimated Selling price | Acceptable Loss price | Profit (or loss) (according to Risk-reward ratio) |
|---|---|---|---|---|
| | | | | |
| | | | | |
| | | | | |
| | | | | |
| | | | | |
| | | | | |
| | | | | |
| | | | | |
| | | | | |
| | | | | |
| | | | | |
| | | | | |
| | | | | |
| | | | | |
| | | | | |
| | | | | |

NOTE:
_____
_____
_____
_____
_____
_____

| Company name: | |
|---|---|
| stock code: | |

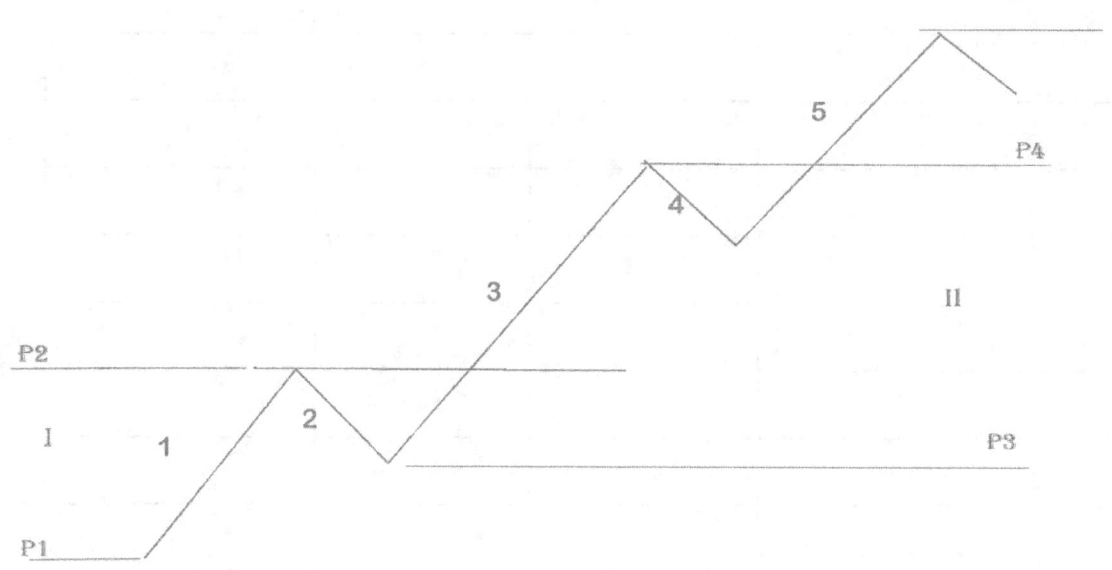

| P4 | I=P2-P1 | |
|---|---|---|
| POSSIBLE | P1+I*1.382= | |
| VALUE | P1+I*1.618= | |

| Risk-reward ratio | Estimated Buying price | Estimated Selling price | Acceptable Loss price | Profit (or loss) (according to Risk-reward ratio) |
|---|---|---|---|---|
| | | | | |
| | | | | |
| | | | | |
| | | | | |
| | | | | |
| | | | | |
| | | | | |
| | | | | |
| | | | | |
| | | | | |
| | | | | |
| | | | | |
| | | | | |
| | | | | |
| | | | | |

NOTE:

| Company name: | |
| --- | --- |
| stock code: | |

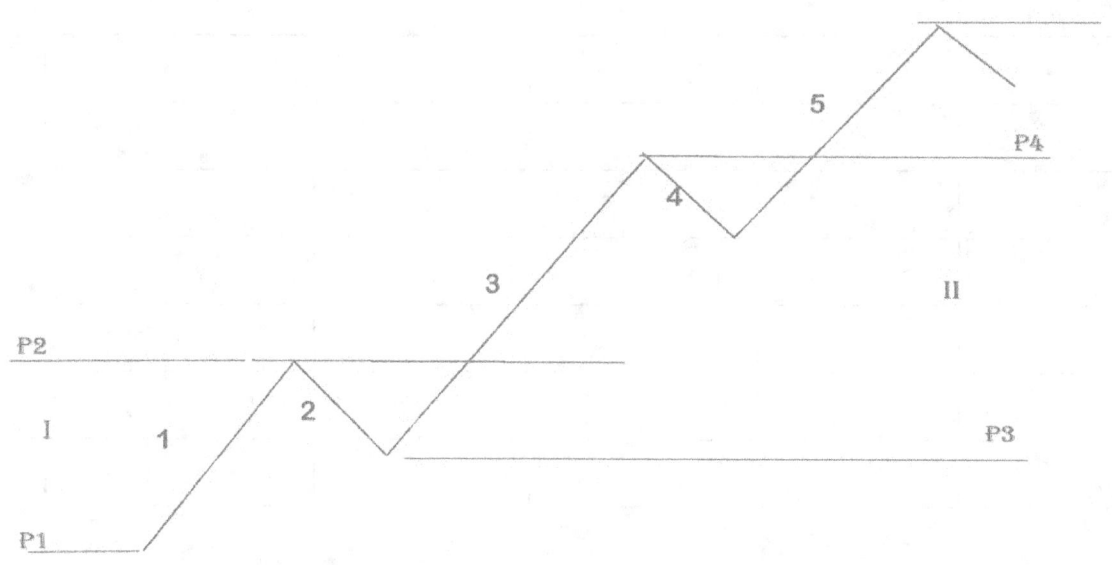

| P4 | I=P2-P1 | |
| --- | --- | --- |
| POSSIBLE | P1+I*1.382= | |
| VALUE | P1+I*1.618= | |

| Risk-reward ratio | Estimated Buying price | Estimated Selling price | Acceptable Loss price | Profit (or loss) (according to Risk-reward ratio) |
|---|---|---|---|---|
| | | | | |
| | | | | |
| | | | | |
| | | | | |
| | | | | |
| | | | | |
| | | | | |
| | | | | |
| | | | | |
| | | | | |
| | | | | |
| | | | | |
| | | | | |
| | | | | |
| | | | | |
| | | | | |
| | | | | |

NOTE:
_____
_____
_____
_____
_____
_____

| Company name: | |
|---|---|
| stock code: | |

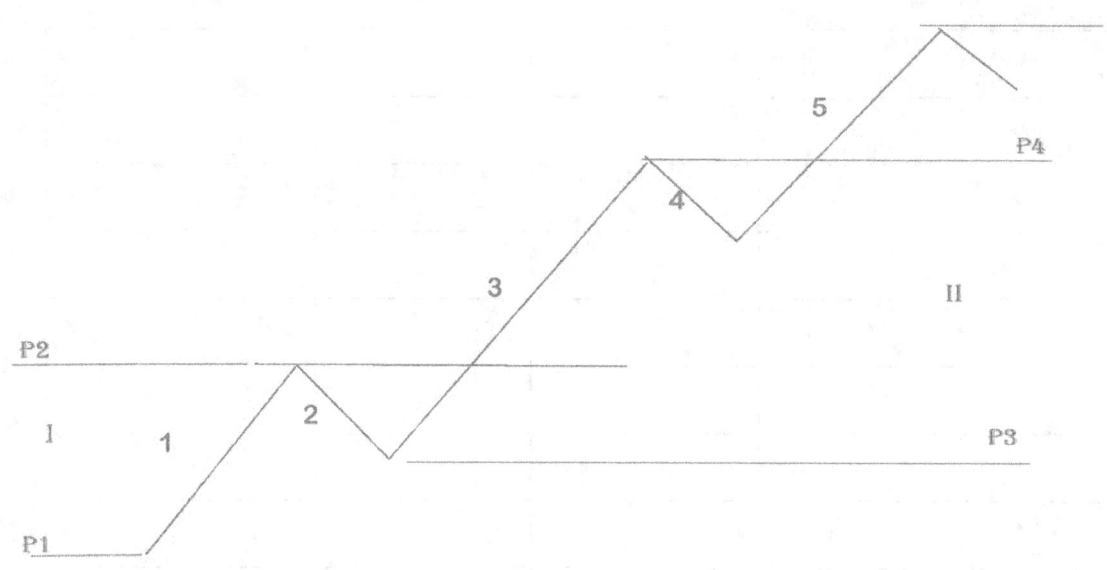

| P4 | I=P2-P1 | |
|---|---|---|
| POSSIBLE | P1+I*1.382= | |
| VALUE | P1+I*1.618= | |

| Risk-reward ratio | Estimated Buying price | Estimated Selling price | Acceptable Loss price | Profit (or loss) (according to Risk-reward ratio) |
|---|---|---|---|---|
| | | | | |
| | | | | |
| | | | | |
| | | | | |
| | | | | |
| | | | | |
| | | | | |
| | | | | |
| | | | | |
| | | | | |
| | | | | |
| | | | | |
| | | | | |
| | | | | |
| | | | | |
| | | | | |

NOTE:

| Company name: | |
|---|---|
| stock code: | |

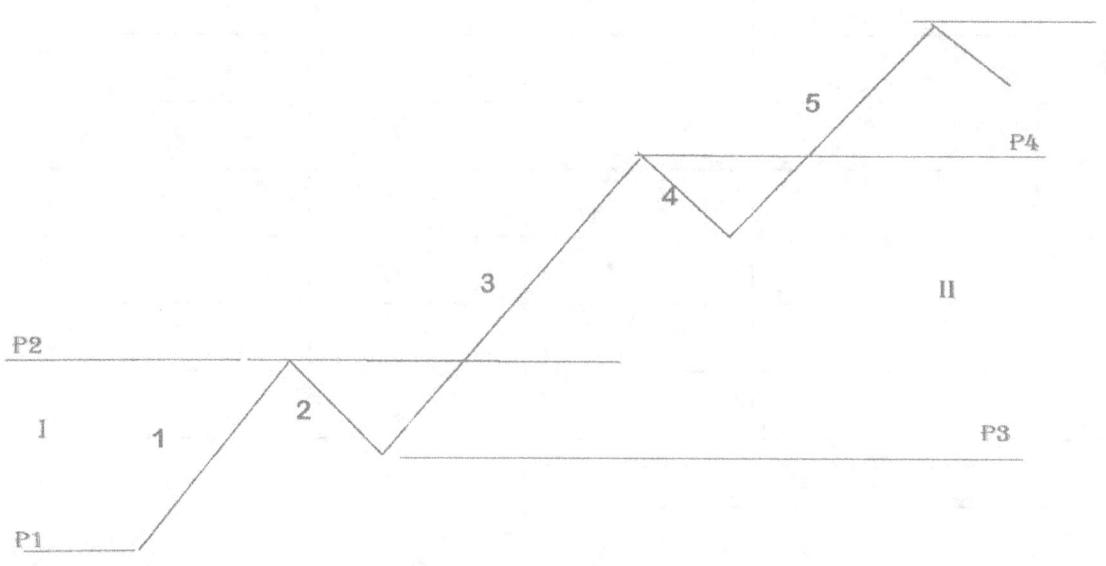

| P4 | I=P2-P1 | |
|---|---|---|
| POSSIBLE | P1+I*1.382= | |
| VALUE | P1+I*1.618= | |

| Risk-reward ratio | Estimated Buying price | Estimated Selling price | Acceptable Loss price | Profit (or loss) (according to Risk-reward ratio) |
|---|---|---|---|---|
| | | | | |
| | | | | |
| | | | | |
| | | | | |
| | | | | |
| | | | | |
| | | | | |
| | | | | |
| | | | | |
| | | | | |
| | | | | |
| | | | | |
| | | | | |
| | | | | |
| | | | | |
| | | | | |

NOTE:
_____
_____
_____
_____
_____
_____
_____

| Company name: | |
|---|---|
| stock code: | |

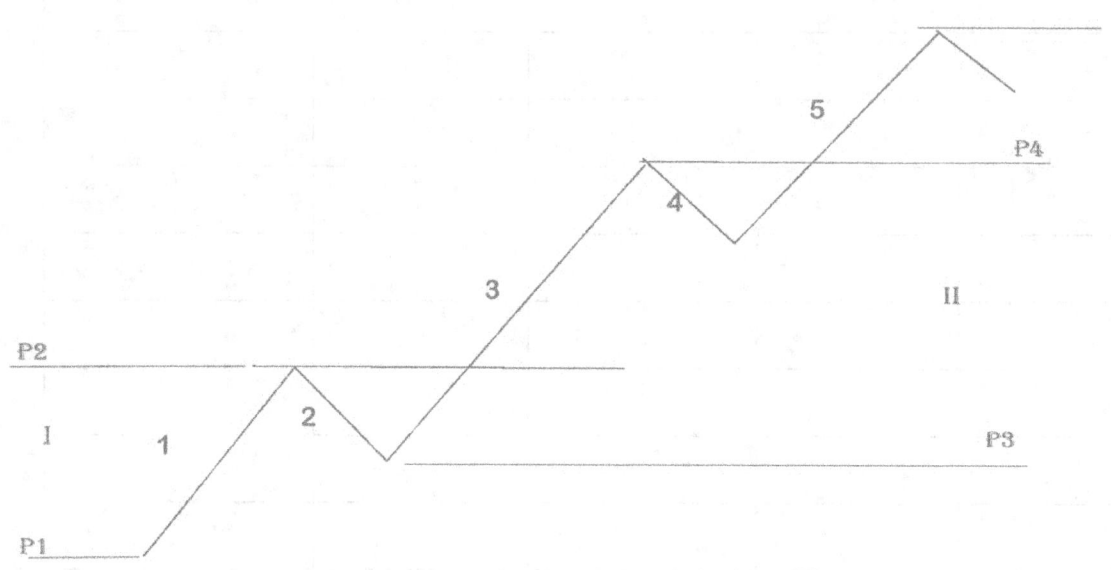

| P4 | I=P2-P1 | |
|---|---|---|
| POSSIBLE | P1+I*1.382= | |
| VALUE | P1+I*1.618= | |

| Risk-reward ratio | Estimated Buying price | Estimated Selling price | Acceptable Loss price | Profit (or loss) (according to Risk-reward ratio) |
|---|---|---|---|---|
| | | | | |
| | | | | |
| | | | | |
| | | | | |
| | | | | |
| | | | | |
| | | | | |
| | | | | |
| | | | | |
| | | | | |
| | | | | |
| | | | | |
| | | | | |
| | | | | |
| | | | | |
| | | | | |

NOTE:

| Company name: | |
|---|---|
| stock code: | |

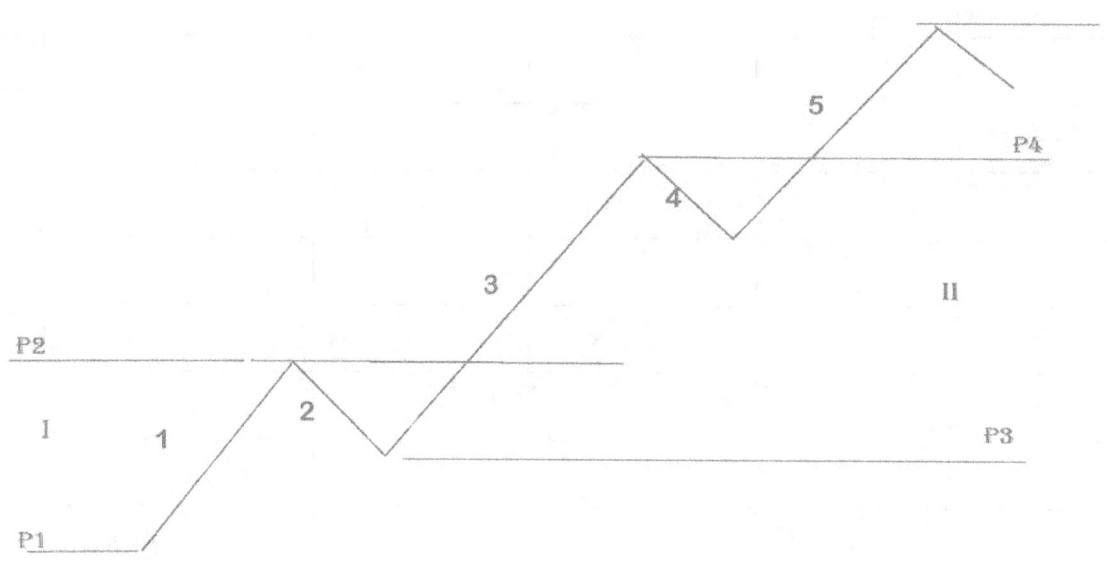

| P4 | I=P2-P1 | |
|---|---|---|
| POSSIBLE | P1+I*1.382= | |
| VALUE | P1+I*1.618= | |

| Risk-reward ratio | Estimated Buying price | Estimated Selling price | Acceptable Loss price | Profit (or loss) (according to Risk-reward ratio) |
|---|---|---|---|---|
| | | | | |
| | | | | |
| | | | | |
| | | | | |
| | | | | |
| | | | | |
| | | | | |
| | | | | |
| | | | | |
| | | | | |
| | | | | |
| | | | | |
| | | | | |
| | | | | |
| | | | | |
| | | | | |

NOTE:

| Company name: | |
|---|---|
| stock code: | |

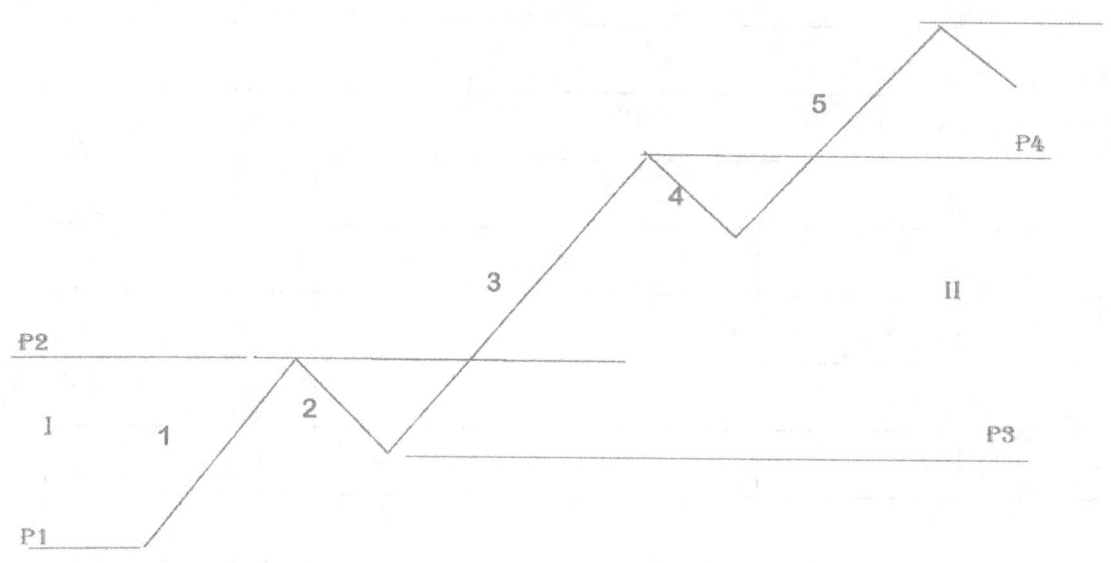

| P4 | I=P2-P1 | |
|---|---|---|
| POSSIBLE | P1+I*1.382= | |
| VALUE | P1+I*1.618= | |

| Risk-reward ratio | Estimated Buying price | Estimated Selling price | Acceptable Loss price | Profit (or loss) (according to Risk-reward ratio) |
|---|---|---|---|---|
| | | | | |
| | | | | |
| | | | | |
| | | | | |
| | | | | |
| | | | | |
| | | | | |
| | | | | |
| | | | | |
| | | | | |
| | | | | |
| | | | | |
| | | | | |
| | | | | |
| | | | | |

NOTE:

| Company name: | |
|---|---|
| stock code: | |

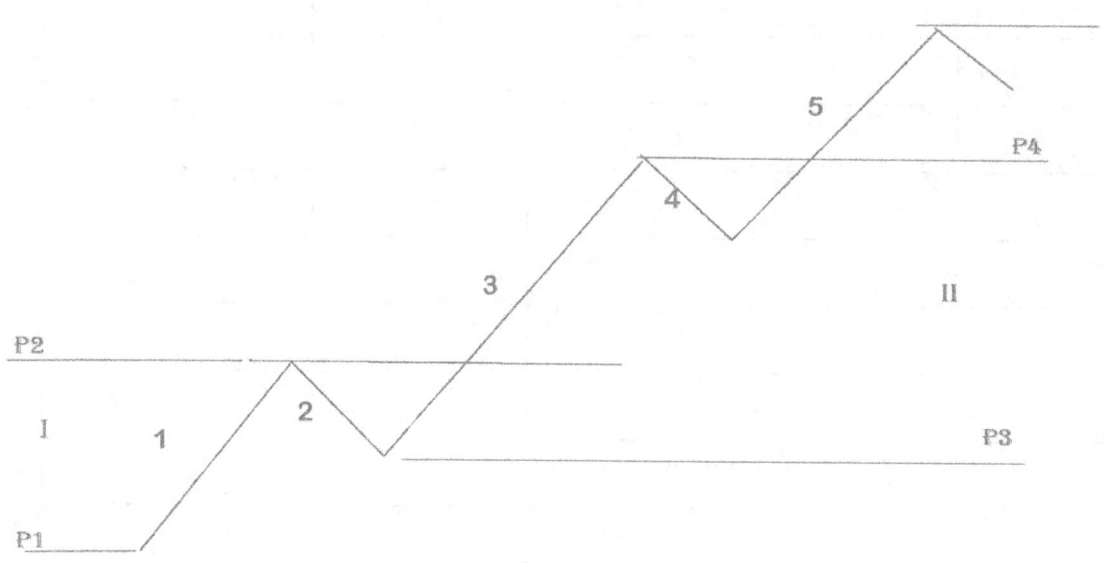

| P4 | I=P2-P1 | |
|---|---|---|
| POSSIBLE | P1+I*1.382= | |
| VALUE | P1+I*1.618= | |

| Risk-reward ratio | Estimated Buying price | Estimated Selling price | Acceptable Loss price | Profit (or loss) (according to Risk-reward ratio) |
|---|---|---|---|---|
| | | | | |
| | | | | |
| | | | | |
| | | | | |
| | | | | |
| | | | | |
| | | | | |
| | | | | |
| | | | | |
| | | | | |
| | | | | |
| | | | | |
| | | | | |
| | | | | |
| | | | | |
| | | | | |
| | | | | |

NOTE:
_____
_____
_____
_____
_____
_____

| Company name: | |
|---|---|
| stock code: | |

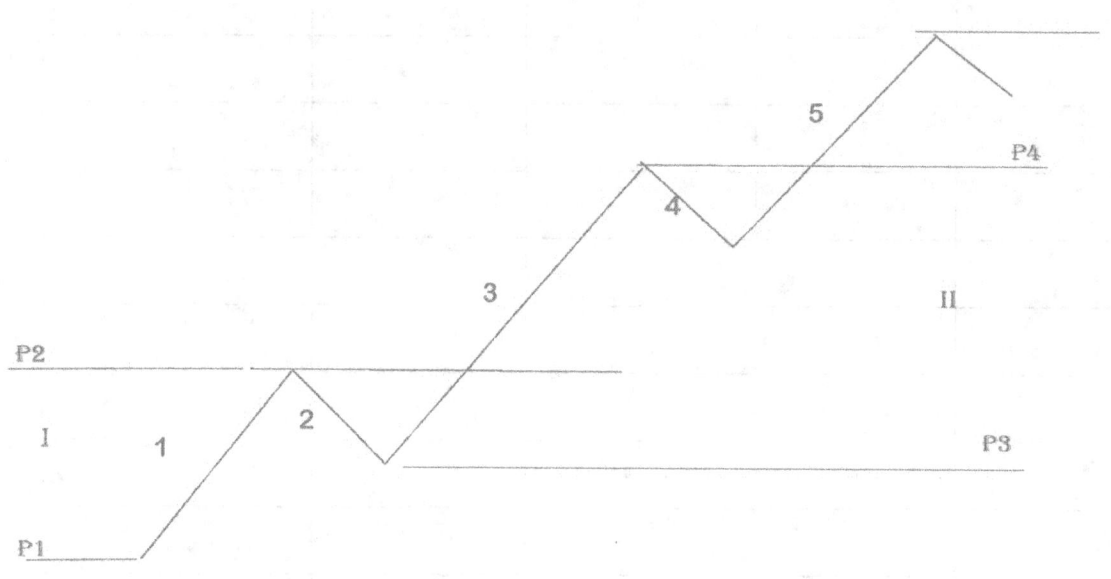

| P4 | I=P2-P1 | |
|---|---|---|
| POSSIBLE | P1+I*1.382= | |
| VALUE | P1+I*1.618= | |

| Risk-reward ratio | Estimated Buying price | Estimated Selling price | Acceptable Loss price | Profit (or loss) (according to Risk-reward ratio) |
|---|---|---|---|---|
|  |  |  |  |  |
|  |  |  |  |  |
|  |  |  |  |  |
|  |  |  |  |  |
|  |  |  |  |  |
|  |  |  |  |  |
|  |  |  |  |  |
|  |  |  |  |  |
|  |  |  |  |  |
|  |  |  |  |  |
|  |  |  |  |  |
|  |  |  |  |  |
|  |  |  |  |  |
|  |  |  |  |  |
|  |  |  |  |  |
|  |  |  |  |  |
|  |  |  |  |  |

NOTE:

# Part Two

## Falling Tendency Cycle

| Company name: | |
|---|---|
| stock code: | |

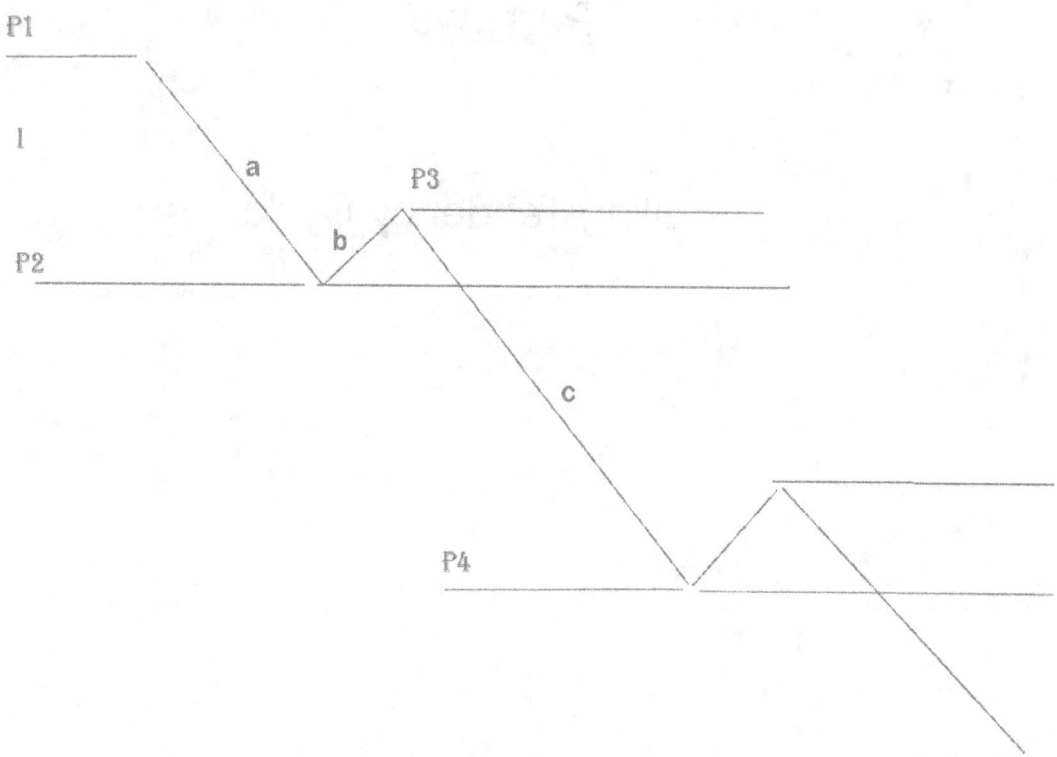

| P4 POSSIBLE VALUE | I=P1-P2 | |
|---|---|---|
| | P1-I*1.382= | |
| | P1-I*1.618= | |

| Risk-reward ratio | Estimated Buying back price | Estimated Overselling price | Acceptable Loss price | Profit (or loss) (according to Risk-reward ratio) |
|---|---|---|---|---|
| | | | | |
| | | | | |
| | | | | |
| | | | | |
| | | | | |
| | | | | |
| | | | | |
| | | | | |
| | | | | |
| | | | | |
| | | | | |
| | | | | |
| | | | | |
| | | | | |
| | | | | |
| | | | | |

NOTE:
_____
_____
_____
_____
_____
_____
_____

| Company name: | |
|---|---|
| stock code: | |

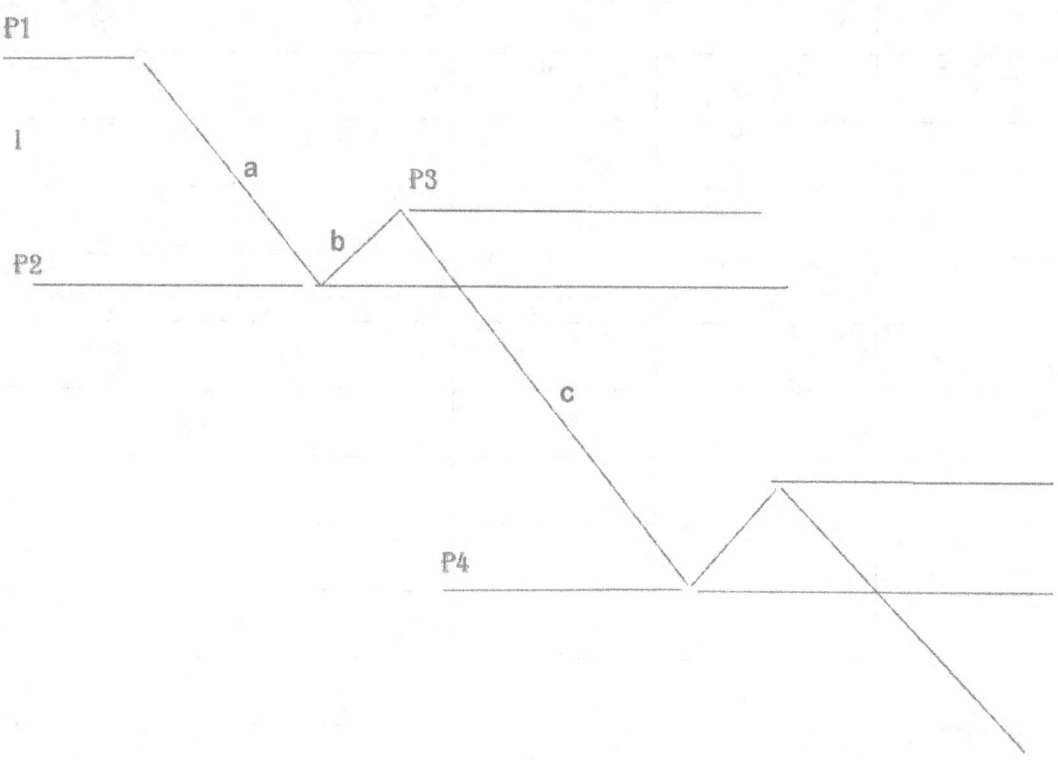

| P4 POSSIBLE VALUE | I=P1-P2 | |
|---|---|---|
| | P1-I*1.382= | |
| | P1-I*1.618= | |

| Risk-reward ratio | Estimated Buying back price | Estimated Overselling price | Acceptable Loss price | Profit (or loss) (according to Risk-reward ratio) |
|---|---|---|---|---|
| | | | | |
| | | | | |
| | | | | |
| | | | | |
| | | | | |
| | | | | |
| | | | | |
| | | | | |
| | | | | |
| | | | | |
| | | | | |
| | | | | |
| | | | | |
| | | | | |
| | | | | |

NOTE:

| Company name: | |
|---|---|
| stock code: | |

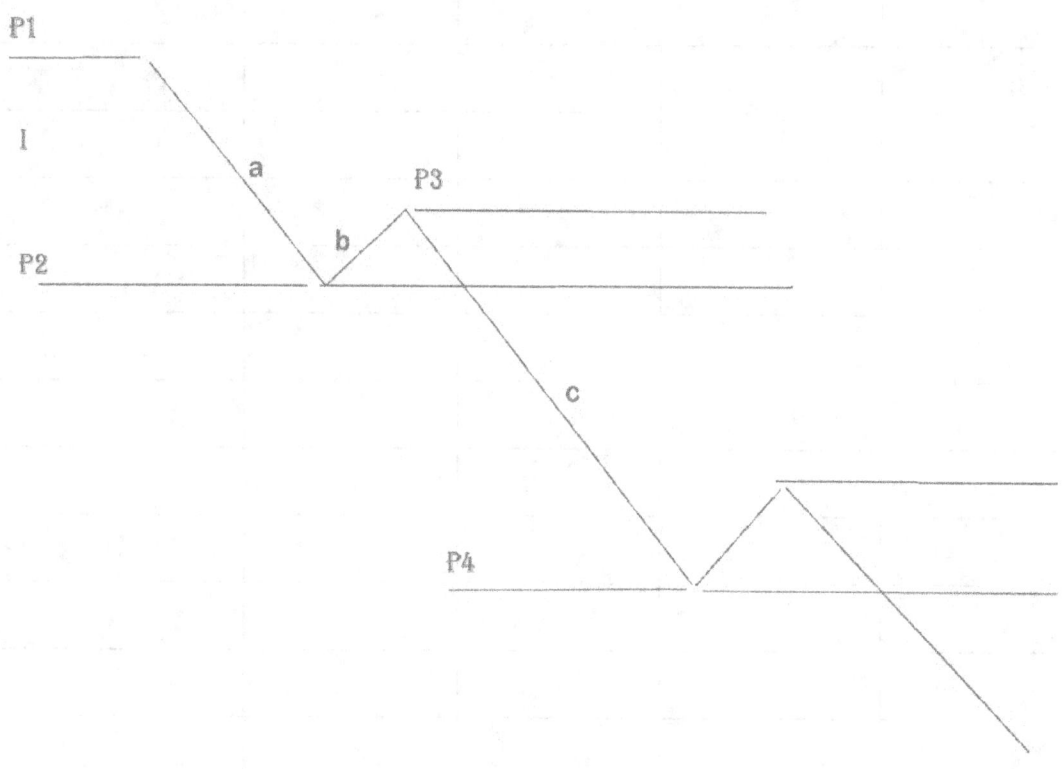

| P4 POSSIBLE VALUE | I=P1-P2 | |
|---|---|---|
| | P1-I*1.382= | |
| | P1-I*1.618= | |

| Risk-reward ratio | Estimated Buying back price | Estimated Overselling price | Acceptable Loss price | Profit (or loss) (according to Risk-reward ratio) |
|---|---|---|---|---|
|  |  |  |  |  |
|  |  |  |  |  |
|  |  |  |  |  |
|  |  |  |  |  |
|  |  |  |  |  |
|  |  |  |  |  |
|  |  |  |  |  |
|  |  |  |  |  |
|  |  |  |  |  |
|  |  |  |  |  |
|  |  |  |  |  |
|  |  |  |  |  |
|  |  |  |  |  |
|  |  |  |  |  |
|  |  |  |  |  |
|  |  |  |  |  |

NOTE:

| Company name: | |
|---|---|
| stock code: | |

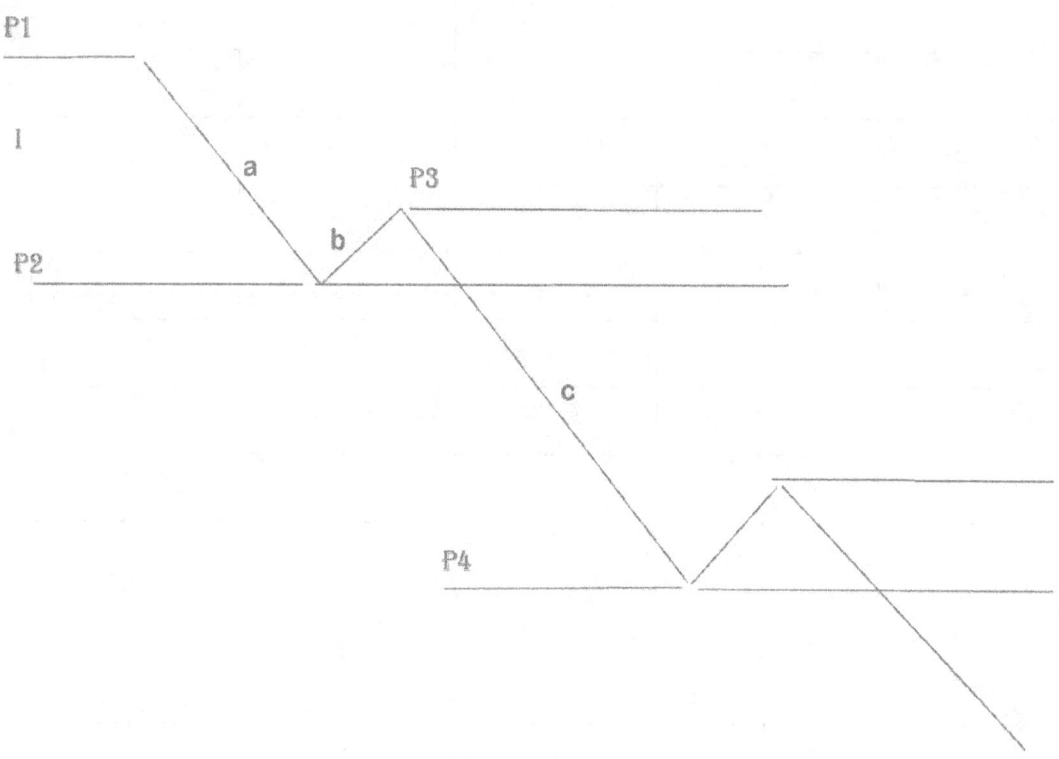

| P4 | I=P1-P2 | |
|---|---|---|
| POSSIBLE | P1-I*1.382= | |
| VALUE | P1-I*1.618= | |

| Risk-reward ratio | Estimated Buying back price | Estimated Overselling price | Acceptable Loss price | Profit (or loss) (according to Risk-reward ratio) |
|---|---|---|---|---|
| | | | | |
| | | | | |
| | | | | |
| | | | | |
| | | | | |
| | | | | |
| | | | | |
| | | | | |
| | | | | |
| | | | | |
| | | | | |
| | | | | |
| | | | | |
| | | | | |
| | | | | |
| | | | | |

NOTE:

| Company name: | |
| --- | --- |
| stock code: | |

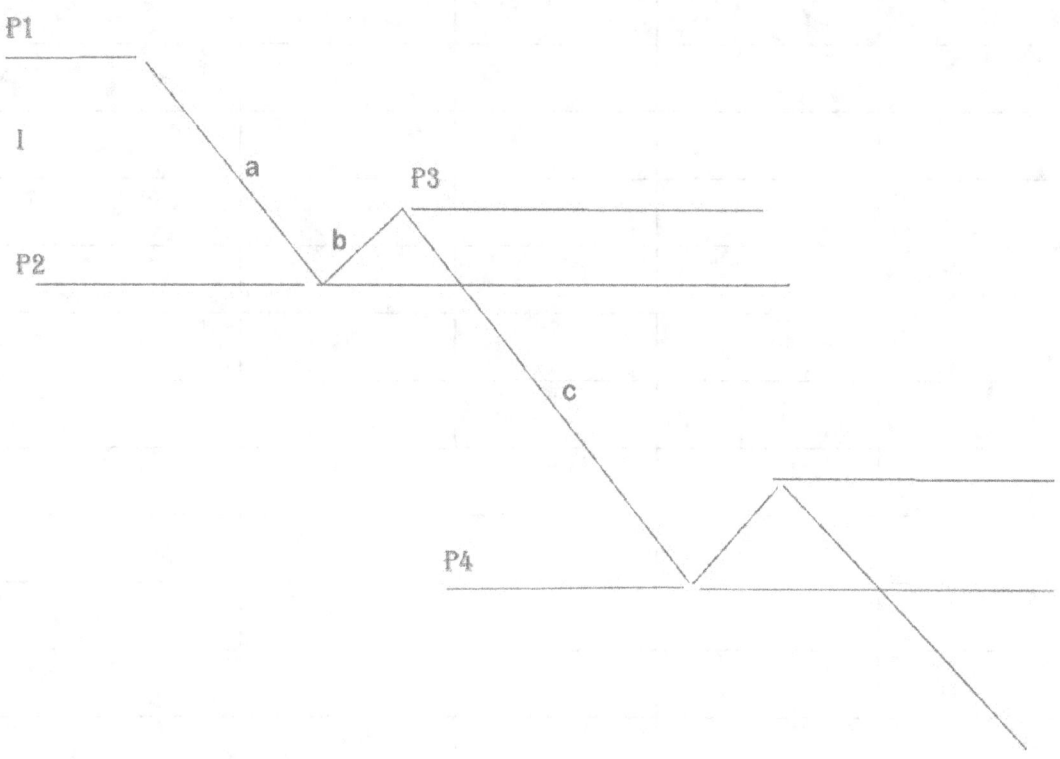

| P4 | I=P1-P2 | |
| --- | --- | --- |
| POSSIBLE | P1-I*1.382= | |
| VALUE | P1-I*1.618= | |

| Risk-reward ratio | Estimated Buying back price | Estimated Overselling price | Acceptable Loss price | Profit (or loss) (according to Risk-reward ratio) |
|---|---|---|---|---|
| | | | | |
| | | | | |
| | | | | |
| | | | | |
| | | | | |
| | | | | |
| | | | | |
| | | | | |
| | | | | |
| | | | | |
| | | | | |
| | | | | |
| | | | | |
| | | | | |
| | | | | |

NOTE:

| Company name: | |
|---|---|
| stock code: | |

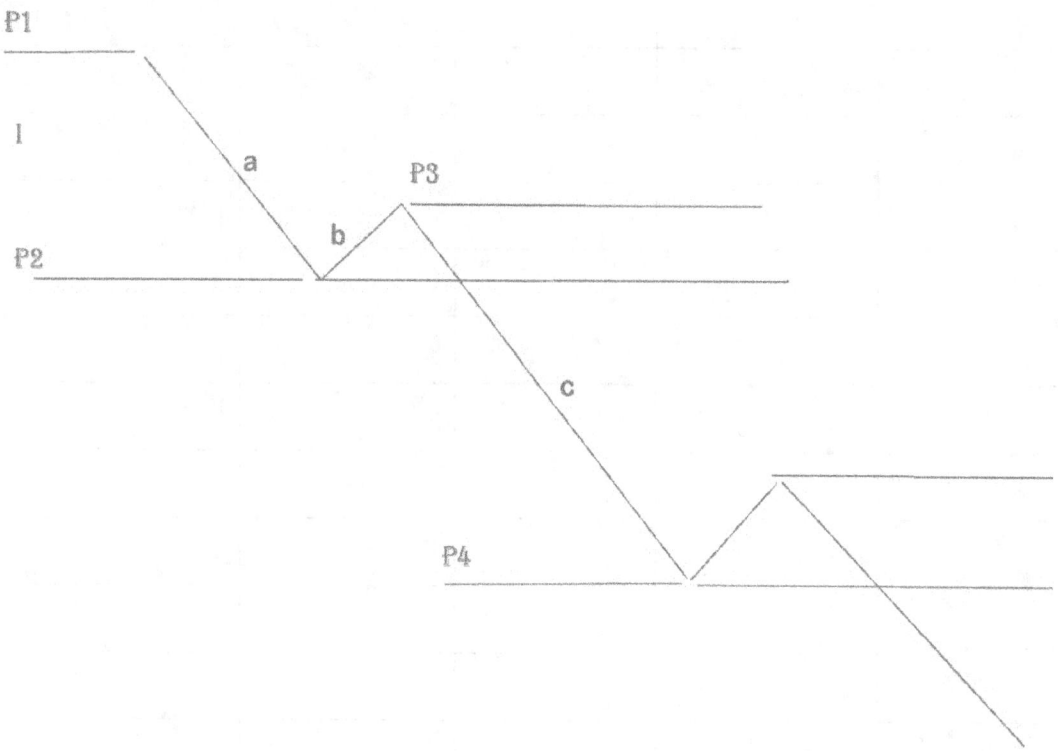

| P4 | I=P1-P2 | |
|---|---|---|
| POSSIBLE | P1-I*1.382= | |
| VALUE | P1-I*1.618= | |

| Risk-reward ratio | Estimated Buying back price | Estimated Overselling price | Acceptable Loss price | Profit (or loss) (according to Risk-reward ratio) |
|---|---|---|---|---|
| | | | | |
| | | | | |
| | | | | |
| | | | | |
| | | | | |
| | | | | |
| | | | | |
| | | | | |
| | | | | |
| | | | | |
| | | | | |
| | | | | |
| | | | | |
| | | | | |
| | | | | |
| | | | | |

NOTE:

| Company name: | |
|---|---|
| stock code: | |

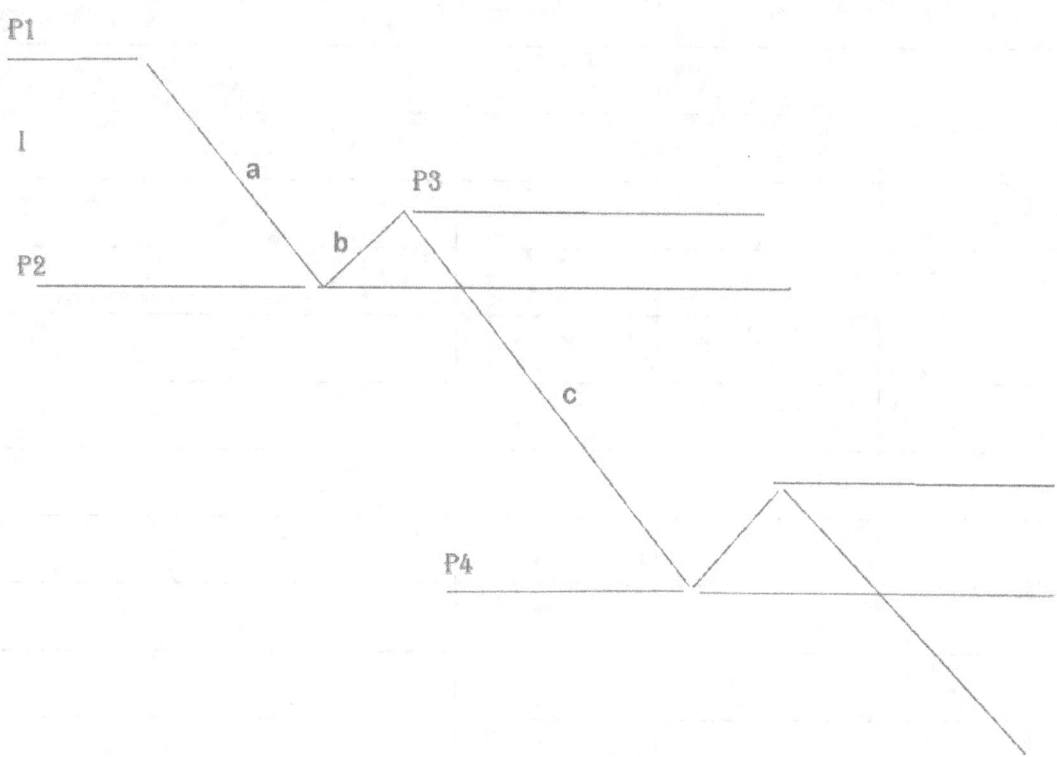

| P4 | I=P1-P2 | |
|---|---|---|
| POSSIBLE | P1-I*1.382= | |
| VALUE | P1-I*1.618= | |

| Risk-reward ratio | Estimated Buying back price | Estimated Overselling price | Acceptable Loss price | Profit (or loss) (according to Risk-reward ratio) |
|---|---|---|---|---|
| | | | | |
| | | | | |
| | | | | |
| | | | | |
| | | | | |
| | | | | |
| | | | | |
| | | | | |
| | | | | |
| | | | | |
| | | | | |
| | | | | |
| | | | | |
| | | | | |
| | | | | |
| | | | | |

NOTE:
___
___
___
___
___
___

| Company name: | |
|---|---|
| stock code: | |

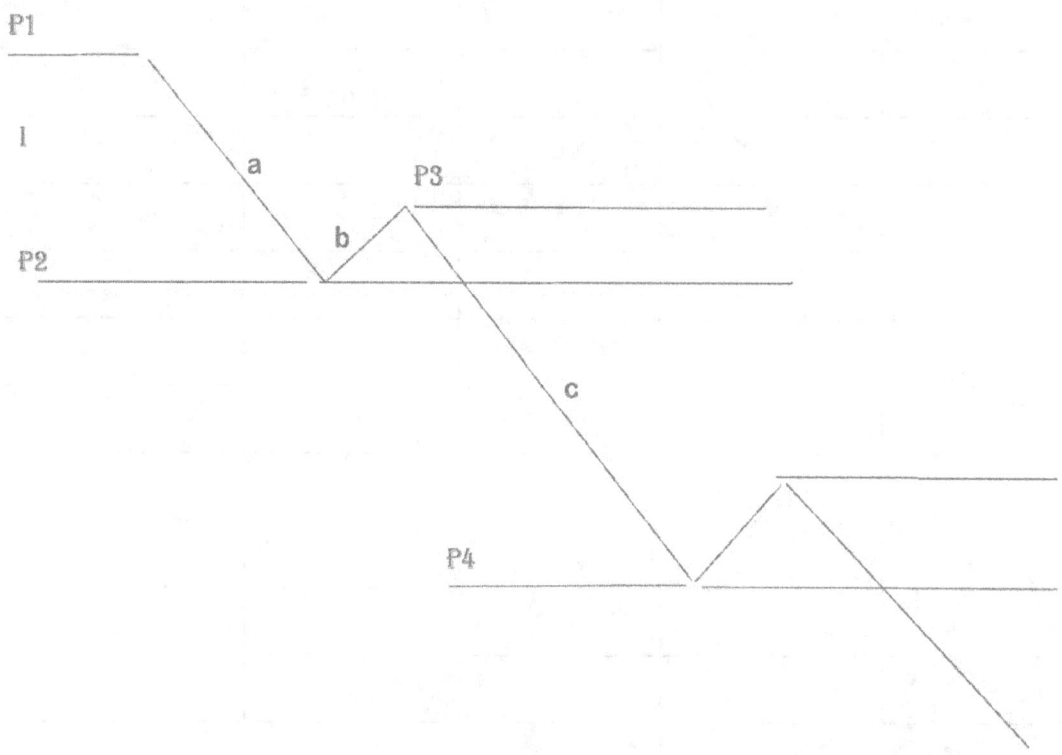

| P4 POSSIBLE VALUE | I=P1-P2 | |
|---|---|---|
| | P1-I*1.382= | |
| | P1-I*1.618= | |

| Risk-reward ratio | Estimated Buying back price | Estimated Overselling price | Acceptable Loss price | Profit (or loss) (according to Risk-reward ratio) |
|---|---|---|---|---|
| | | | | |
| | | | | |
| | | | | |
| | | | | |
| | | | | |
| | | | | |
| | | | | |
| | | | | |
| | | | | |
| | | | | |
| | | | | |
| | | | | |
| | | | | |
| | | | | |
| | | | | |
| | | | | |

NOTE:

| Company name: | |
| --- | --- |
| stock code: | |

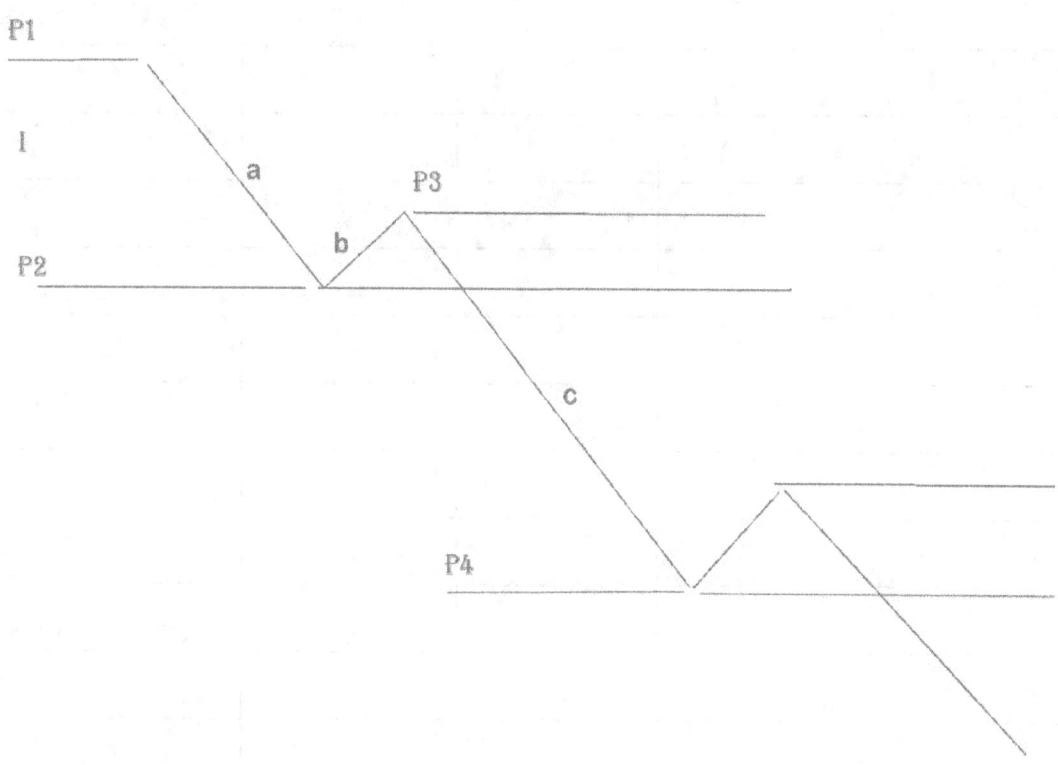

| P4 | I=P1-P2 | |
| --- | --- | --- |
| POSSIBLE | P1-I*1.382= | |
| VALUE | P1-I*1.618= | |

| Risk-reward ratio | Estimated Buying back price | Estimated Overselling price | Acceptable Loss price | Profit (or loss) (according to Risk-reward ratio) |
|---|---|---|---|---|
| | | | | |
| | | | | |
| | | | | |
| | | | | |
| | | | | |
| | | | | |
| | | | | |
| | | | | |
| | | | | |
| | | | | |
| | | | | |
| | | | | |
| | | | | |
| | | | | |
| | | | | |
| | | | | |

NOTE:
_____
_____
_____
_____
_____
_____
_____

| Company name: | |
|---|---|
| stock code: | |

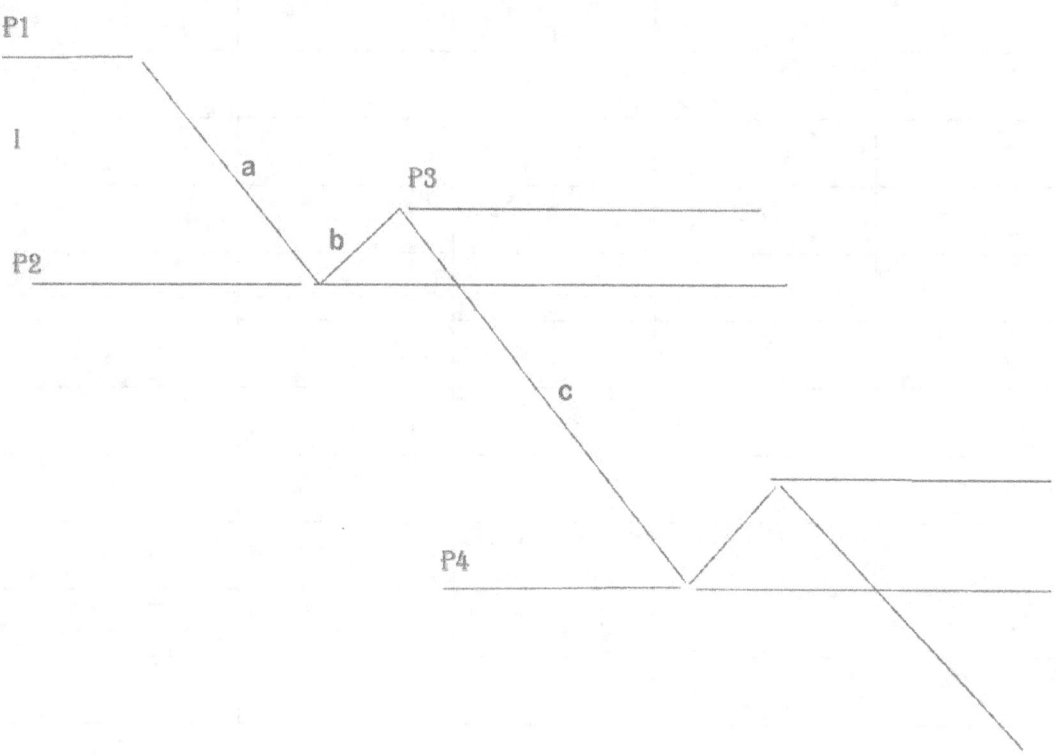

| P4 | I=P1-P2 | |
|---|---|---|
| POSSIBLE | P1-I*1.382= | |
| VALUE | P1-I*1.618= | |

| Risk-reward ratio | Estimated Buying back price | Estimated Overselling price | Acceptable Loss price | Profit (or loss) (according to Risk-reward ratio) |
|---|---|---|---|---|
| | | | | |
| | | | | |
| | | | | |
| | | | | |
| | | | | |
| | | | | |
| | | | | |
| | | | | |
| | | | | |
| | | | | |
| | | | | |
| | | | | |
| | | | | |
| | | | | |
| | | | | |
| | | | | |

NOTE:

| Company name: | |
|---|---|
| stock code: | |

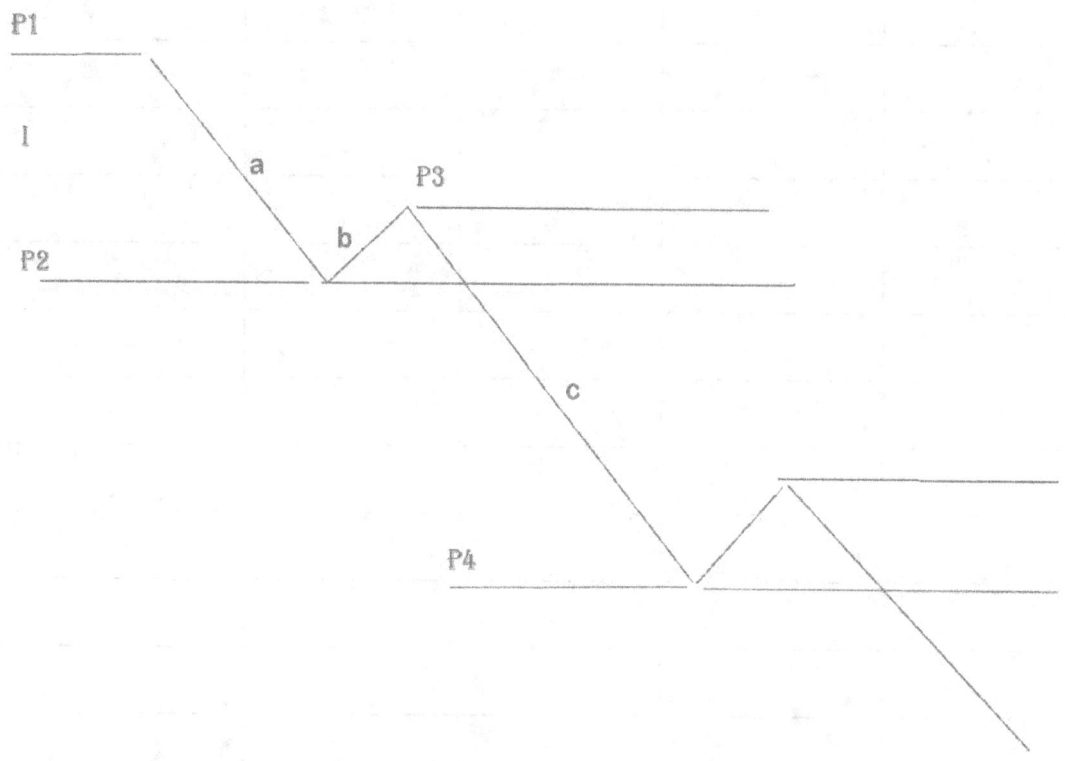

| P4 | I=P1-P2 | |
|---|---|---|
| POSSIBLE | P1-I*1.382= | |
| VALUE | P1-I*1.618= | |

| Risk-reward ratio | Estimated Buying back price | Estimated Overselling price | Acceptable Loss price | Profit (or loss) (according to Risk-reward ratio) |
|---|---|---|---|---|
| | | | | |
| | | | | |
| | | | | |
| | | | | |
| | | | | |
| | | | | |
| | | | | |
| | | | | |
| | | | | |
| | | | | |
| | | | | |
| | | | | |
| | | | | |
| | | | | |
| | | | | |
| | | | | |

NOTE:

| Company name: | |
|---|---|
| stock code: | |

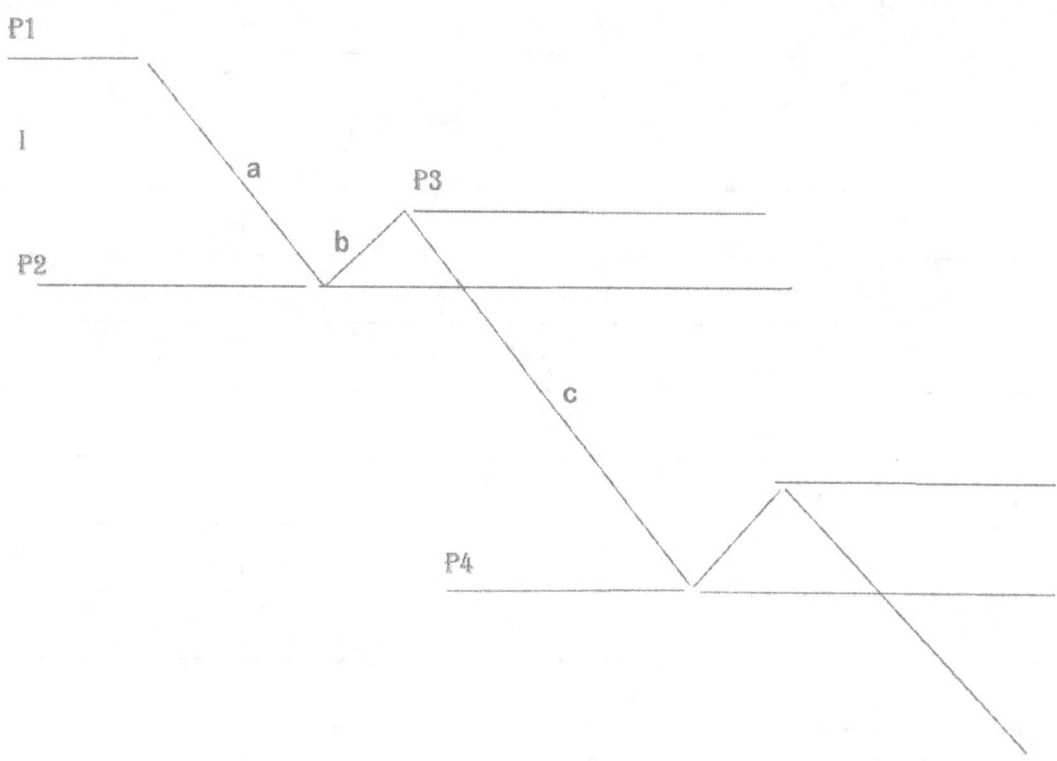

| P4 | I=P1-P2 | |
|---|---|---|
| POSSIBLE | P1-I*1.382= | |
| VALUE | P1-I*1.618= | |

| Risk-reward ratio | Estimated Buying back price | Estimated Overselling price | Acceptable Loss price | Profit (or loss) (according to Risk-reward ratio) |
|---|---|---|---|---|
| | | | | |
| | | | | |
| | | | | |
| | | | | |
| | | | | |
| | | | | |
| | | | | |
| | | | | |
| | | | | |
| | | | | |
| | | | | |
| | | | | |
| | | | | |
| | | | | |
| | | | | |
| | | | | |

NOTE:
_____
_____
_____
_____
_____
_____

| Company name: | |
| --- | --- |
| stock code: | |

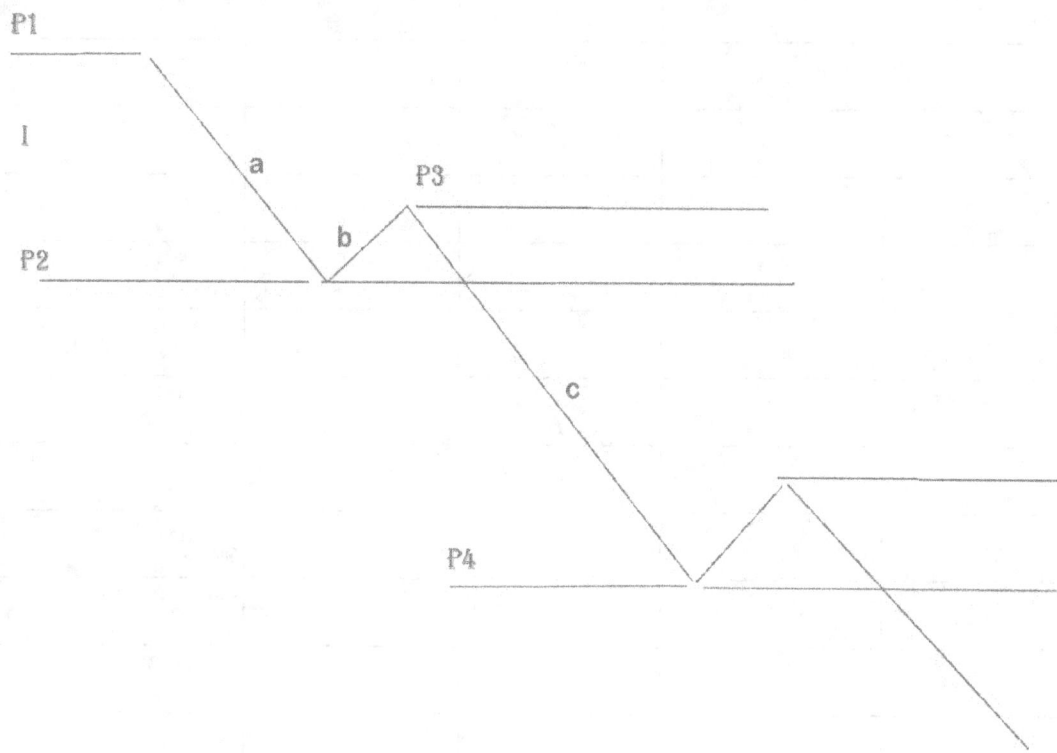

| P4 | I=P1-P2 | |
| --- | --- | --- |
| POSSIBLE | P1-I*1.382= | |
| VALUE | P1-I*1.618= | |

| Risk-reward ratio | Estimated Buying back price | Estimated Overselling price | Acceptable Loss price | Profit (or loss) (according to Risk-reward ratio) |
|---|---|---|---|---|
| | | | | |
| | | | | |
| | | | | |
| | | | | |
| | | | | |
| | | | | |
| | | | | |
| | | | | |
| | | | | |
| | | | | |
| | | | | |
| | | | | |
| | | | | |
| | | | | |
| | | | | |
| | | | | |

NOTE:
_____
_____
_____
_____
_____
_____
_____

| Company name: | |
|---|---|
| stock code: | |

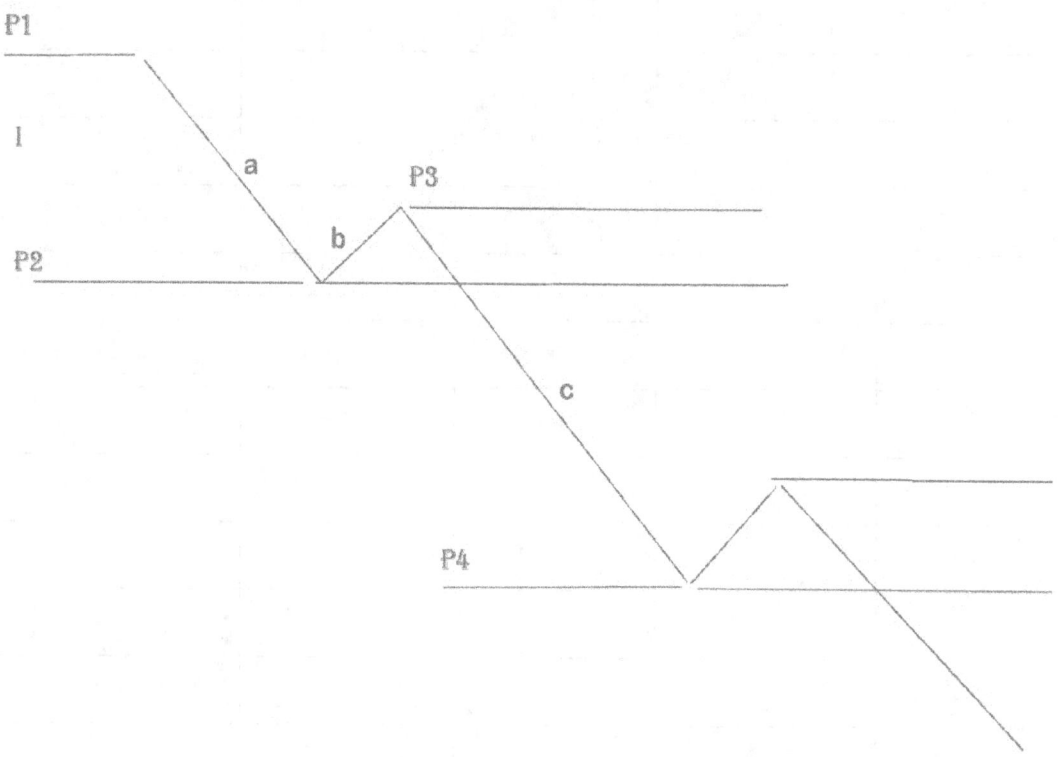

| P4 | I=P1-P2 | |
|---|---|---|
| POSSIBLE | P1-I*1.382= | |
| VALUE | P1-I*1.618= | |

| Risk-reward ratio | Estimated Buying back price | Estimated Overselling price | Acceptable Loss price | Profit (or loss) (according to Risk-reward ratio) |
|---|---|---|---|---|
| | | | | |
| | | | | |
| | | | | |
| | | | | |
| | | | | |
| | | | | |
| | | | | |
| | | | | |
| | | | | |
| | | | | |
| | | | | |
| | | | | |
| | | | | |
| | | | | |
| | | | | |
| | | | | |

NOTE:

| Company name: | |
|---|---|
| stock code: | |

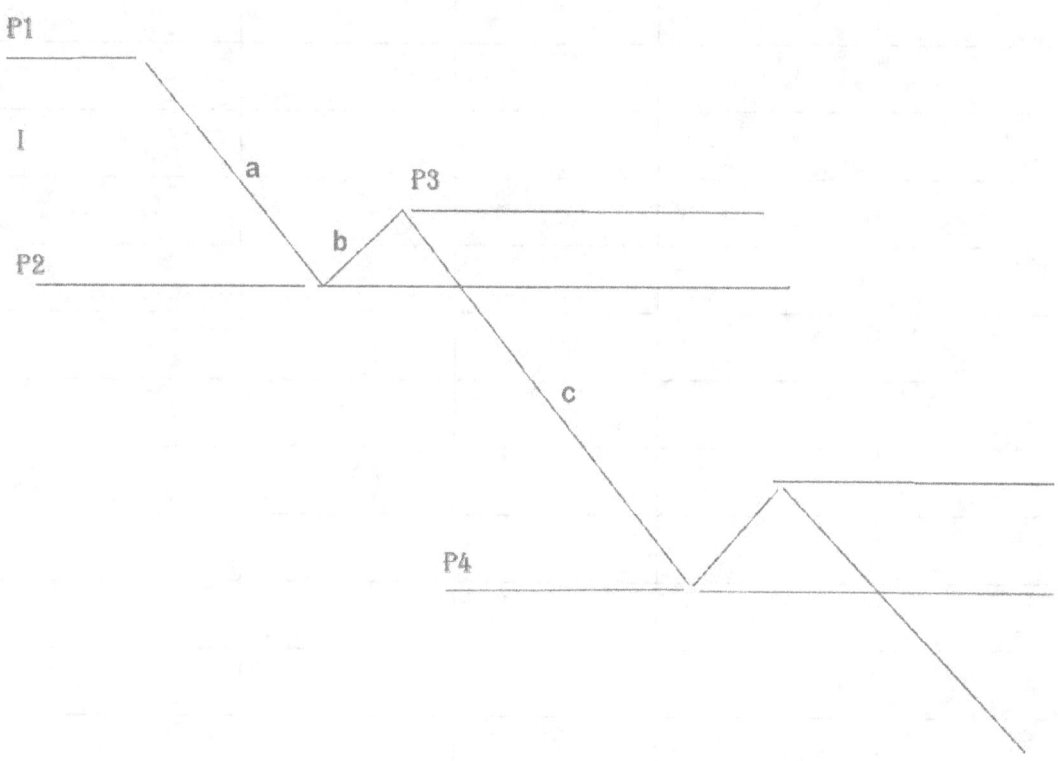

| P4 | I=P1-P2 | |
|---|---|---|
| POSSIBLE | P1-I*1.382= | |
| VALUE | P1-I*1.618= | |

| Risk-reward ratio | Estimated Buying back price | Estimated Overselling price | Acceptable Loss price | Profit (or loss) (according to Risk-reward ratio) |
|---|---|---|---|---|
| | | | | |
| | | | | |
| | | | | |
| | | | | |
| | | | | |
| | | | | |
| | | | | |
| | | | | |
| | | | | |
| | | | | |
| | | | | |
| | | | | |
| | | | | |
| | | | | |
| | | | | |
| | | | | |

NOTE:

| Company name: | |
|---|---|
| stock code: | |

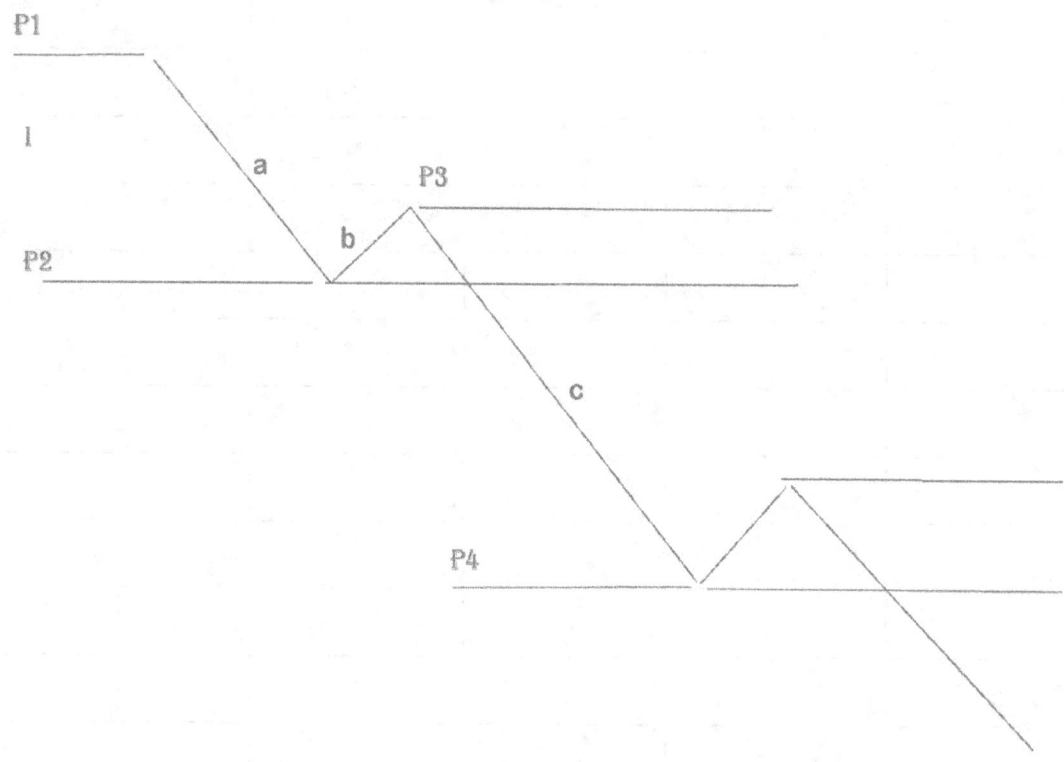

| P4 POSSIBLE VALUE | I=P1-P2 | |
|---|---|---|
| | P1-I*1.382= | |
| | P1-I*1.618= | |

| Risk-reward ratio | Estimated Buying back price | Estimated Overselling price | Acceptable Loss price | Profit (or loss) (according to Risk-reward ratio) |
|---|---|---|---|---|
| | | | | |
| | | | | |
| | | | | |
| | | | | |
| | | | | |
| | | | | |
| | | | | |
| | | | | |
| | | | | |
| | | | | |
| | | | | |
| | | | | |
| | | | | |
| | | | | |
| | | | | |
| | | | | |

NOTE:
_____
_____
_____
_____
_____
_____

| Company name: | |
|---|---|
| stock code: | |

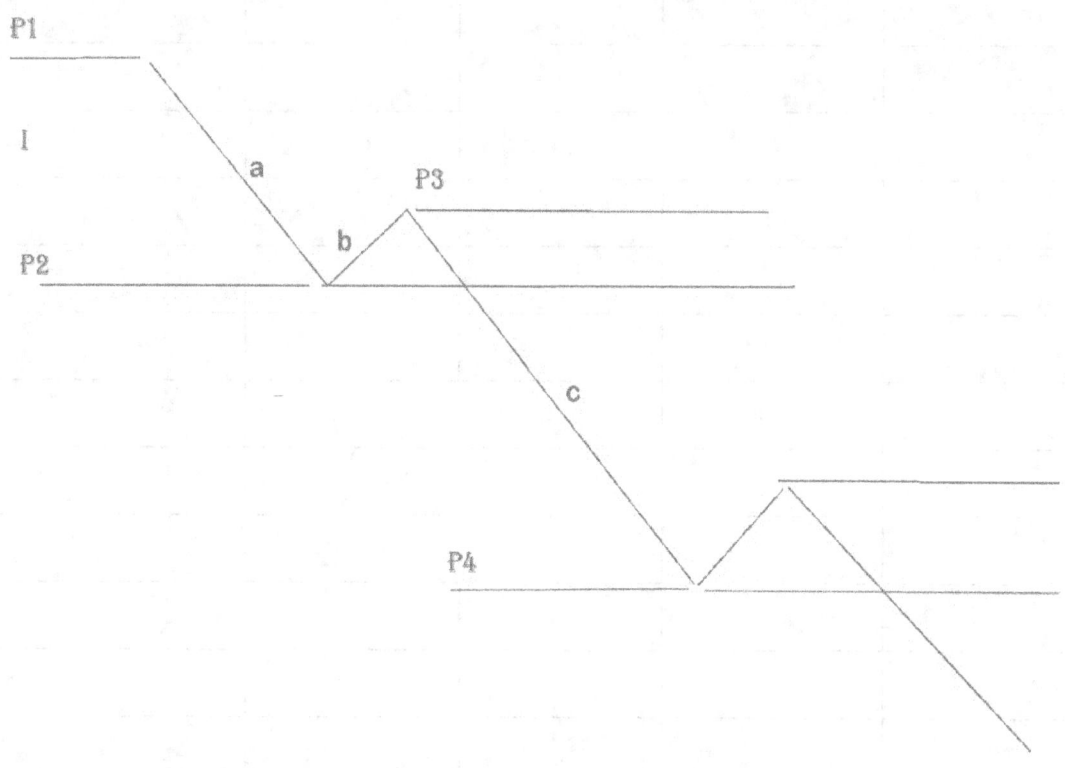

| P4 | I=P1-P2 | |
|---|---|---|
| POSSIBLE | P1-I*1.382= | |
| VALUE | P1-I*1.618= | |

| Risk-reward ratio | Estimated Buying back price | Estimated Overselling price | Acceptable Loss price | Profit (or loss) (according to Risk-reward ratio) |
|---|---|---|---|---|
| | | | | |
| | | | | |
| | | | | |
| | | | | |
| | | | | |
| | | | | |
| | | | | |
| | | | | |
| | | | | |
| | | | | |
| | | | | |
| | | | | |
| | | | | |
| | | | | |
| | | | | |
| | | | | |

NOTE:

| Company name: | |
|---|---|
| stock code: | |

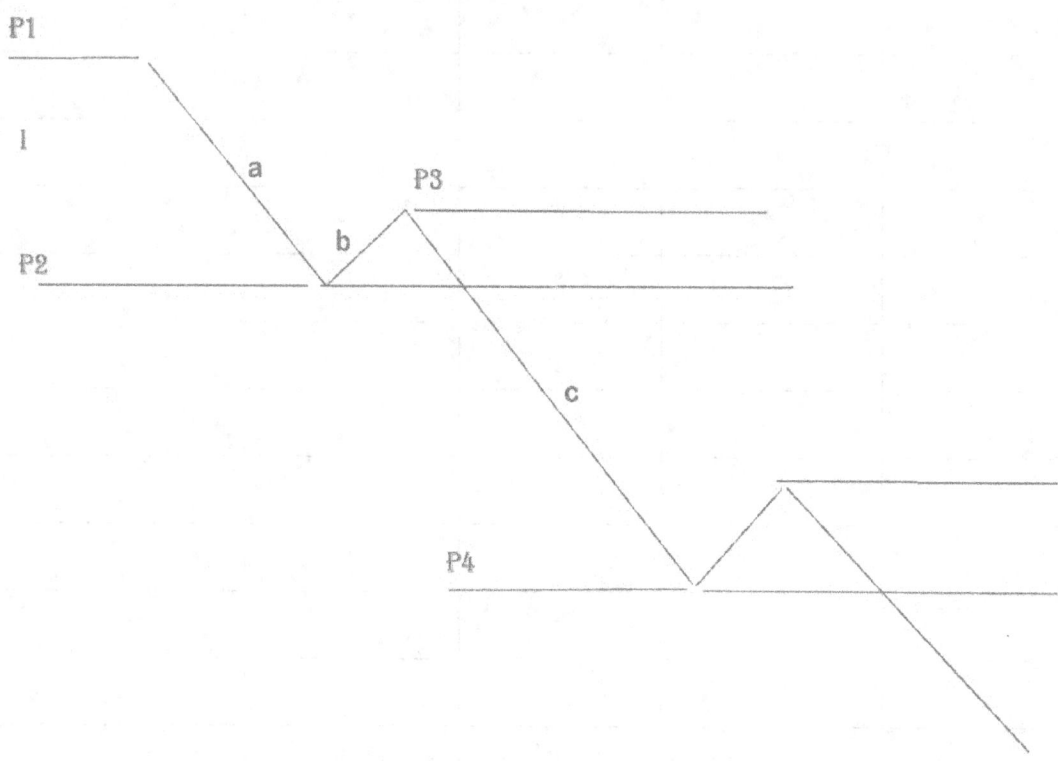

| P4 POSSIBLE VALUE | I=P1-P2 | |
|---|---|---|
| | P1-I*1.382= | |
| | P1-I*1.618= | |

| Risk-reward ratio | Estimated Buying back price | Estimated Overselling price | Acceptable Loss price | Profit (or loss) (according to Risk-reward ratio) |
|---|---|---|---|---|
| | | | | |
| | | | | |
| | | | | |
| | | | | |
| | | | | |
| | | | | |
| | | | | |
| | | | | |
| | | | | |
| | | | | |
| | | | | |
| | | | | |
| | | | | |
| | | | | |
| | | | | |
| | | | | |
| | | | | |

NOTE:
_____
_____
_____
_____
_____
_____
_____

| Company name: | |
| --- | --- |
| stock code: | |

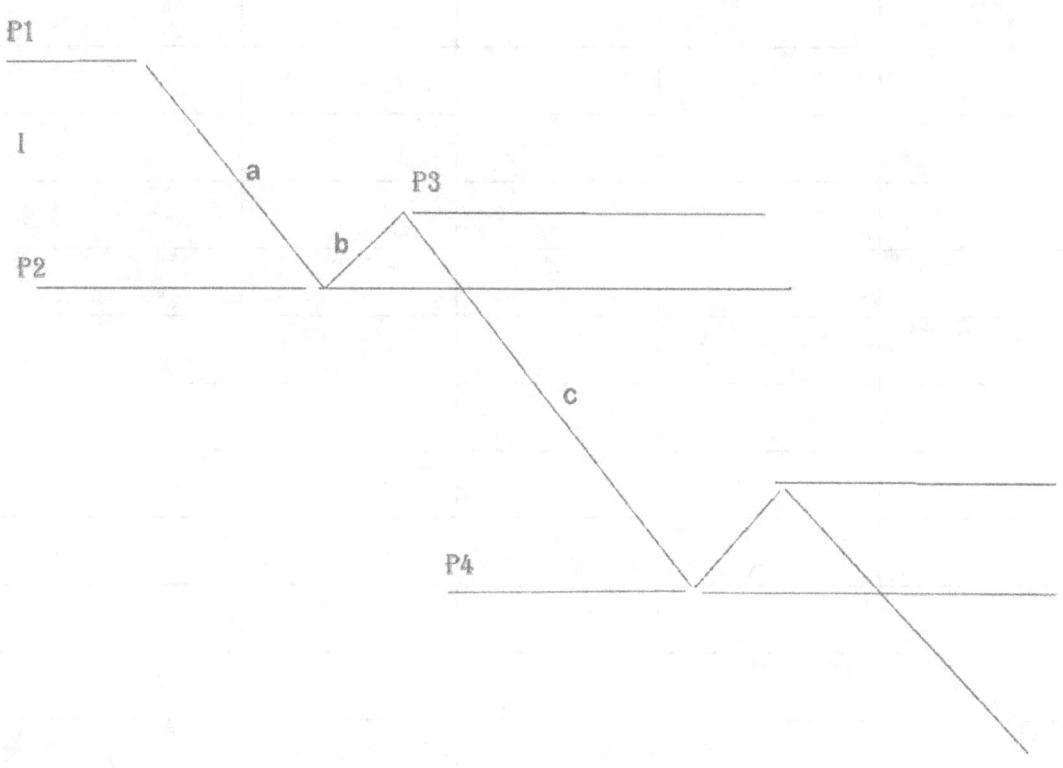

| P4 | I=P1-P2 | |
| --- | --- | --- |
| POSSIBLE | P1-I*1.382= | |
| VALUE | P1-I*1.618= | |

| Risk-reward ratio | Estimated Buying back price | Estimated Overselling price | Acceptable Loss price | Profit (or loss) (according to Risk-reward ratio) |
|---|---|---|---|---|
| | | | | |
| | | | | |
| | | | | |
| | | | | |
| | | | | |
| | | | | |
| | | | | |
| | | | | |
| | | | | |
| | | | | |
| | | | | |
| | | | | |
| | | | | |
| | | | | |
| | | | | |

NOTE:

| Company name: | |
|---|---|
| stock code: | |

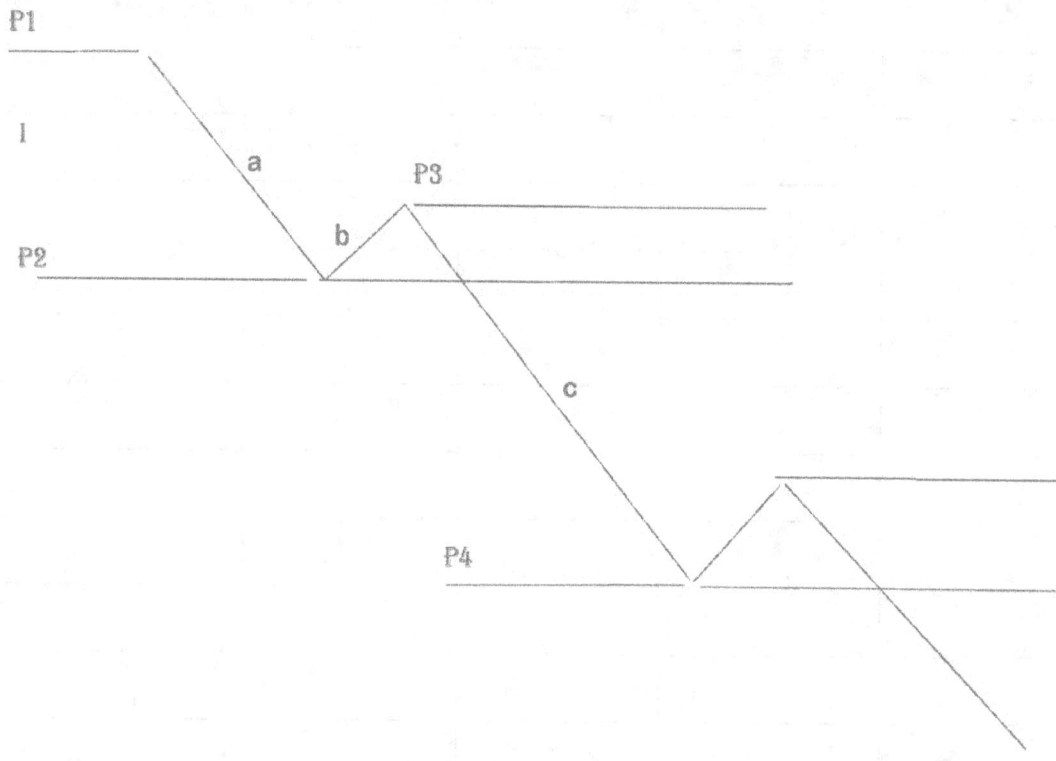

| P4 | I=P1-P2 | |
|---|---|---|
| POSSIBLE | P1-I*1.382= | |
| VALUE | P1-I*1.618= | |

| Risk-reward ratio | Estimated Buying back price | Estimated Overselling price | Acceptable Loss price | Profit (or loss) (according to Risk-reward ratio) |
|---|---|---|---|---|
| | | | | |
| | | | | |
| | | | | |
| | | | | |
| | | | | |
| | | | | |
| | | | | |
| | | | | |
| | | | | |
| | | | | |
| | | | | |
| | | | | |
| | | | | |
| | | | | |
| | | | | |
| | | | | |

NOTE:

| Company name: | |
| --- | --- |
| stock code: | |

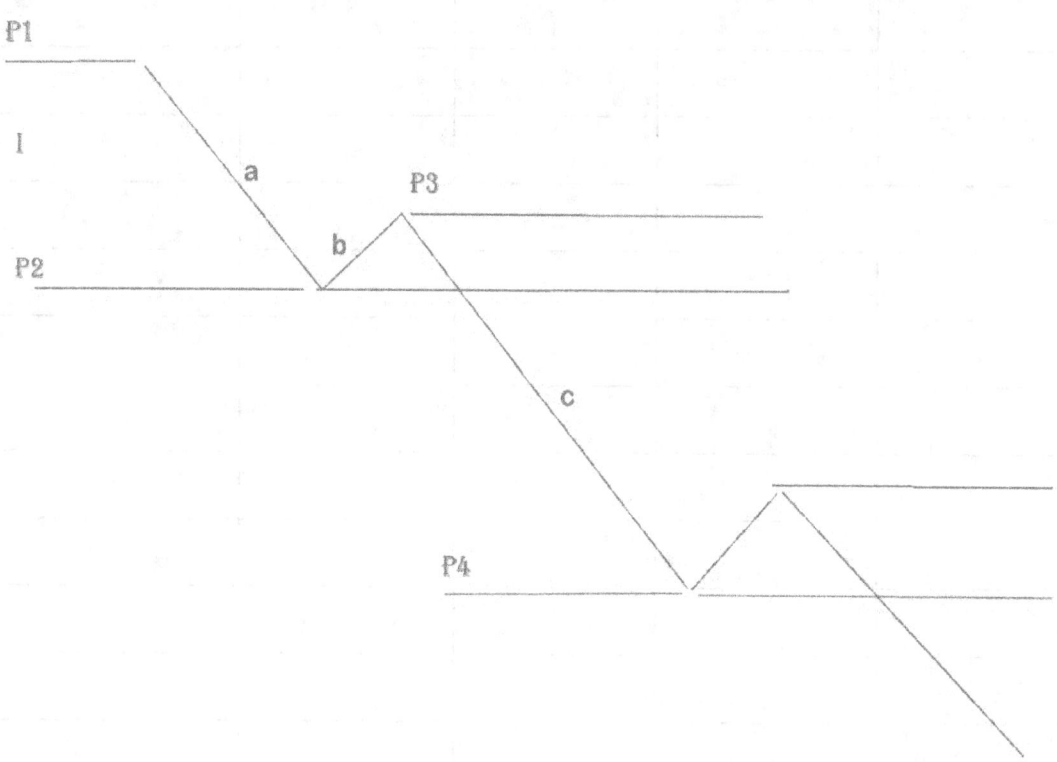

| P4 | I=P1-P2 | |
| --- | --- | --- |
| POSSIBLE | P1-I*1.382= | |
| VALUE | P1-I*1.618= | |

| Risk-reward ratio | Estimated Buying back price | Estimated Overselling price | Acceptable Loss price | Profit (or loss) (according to Risk-reward ratio) |
|---|---|---|---|---|
| | | | | |
| | | | | |
| | | | | |
| | | | | |
| | | | | |
| | | | | |
| | | | | |
| | | | | |
| | | | | |
| | | | | |
| | | | | |
| | | | | |
| | | | | |
| | | | | |
| | | | | |
| | | | | |

NOTE:

| Company name: | |
|---|---|
| stock code: | |

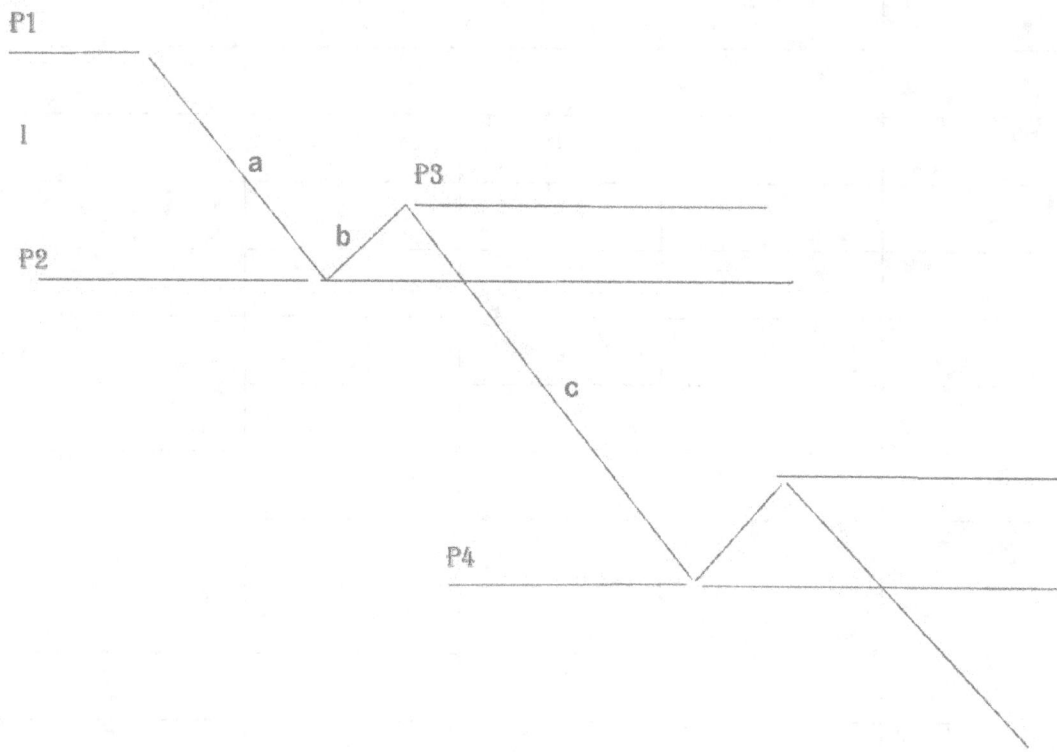

| P4 | I=P1-P2 | |
|---|---|---|
| POSSIBLE | P1-I*1.382= | |
| VALUE | P1-I*1.618= | |

| Risk-reward ratio | Estimated Buying back price | Estimated Overselling price | Acceptable Loss price | Profit (or loss) (according to Risk-reward ratio) |
|---|---|---|---|---|
| | | | | |
| | | | | |
| | | | | |
| | | | | |
| | | | | |
| | | | | |
| | | | | |
| | | | | |
| | | | | |
| | | | | |
| | | | | |
| | | | | |
| | | | | |
| | | | | |
| | | | | |
| | | | | |

NOTE:

| Company name: | |
|---|---|
| stock code: | |

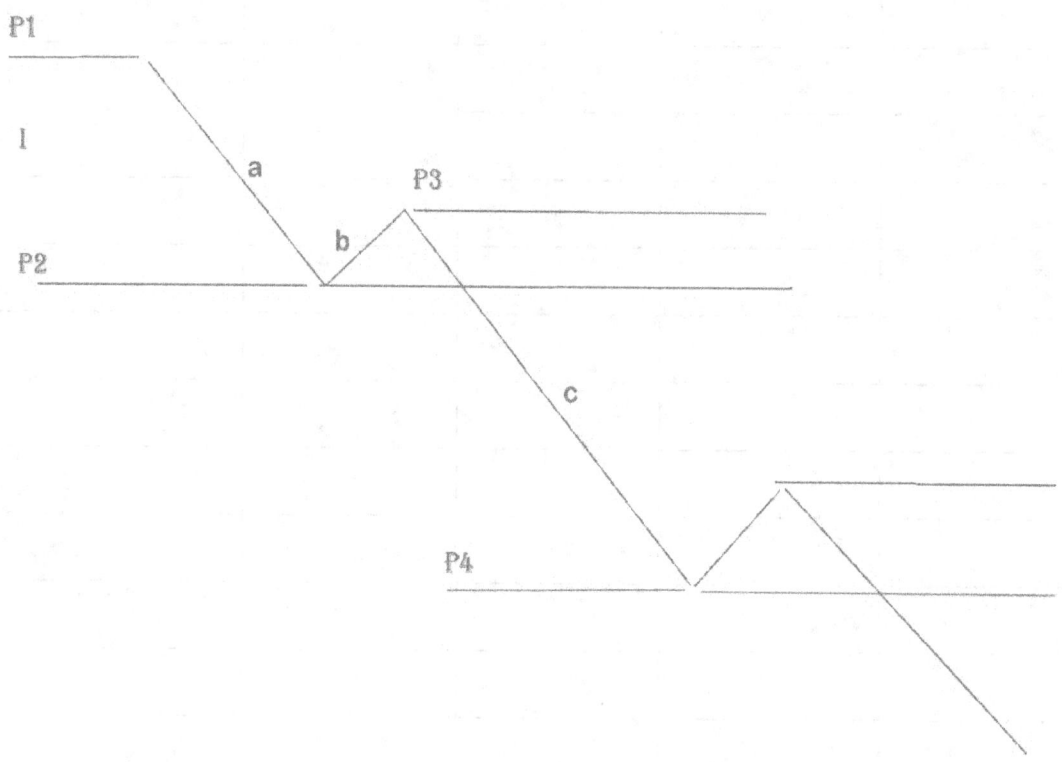

| P4 | I=P1-P2 | |
|---|---|---|
| POSSIBLE | P1-I*1.382= | |
| VALUE | P1-I*1.618= | |

| Risk-reward ratio | Estimated Buying back price | Estimated Overselling price | Acceptable Loss price | Profit (or loss) (according to Risk-reward ratio) |
|---|---|---|---|---|
| | | | | |
| | | | | |
| | | | | |
| | | | | |
| | | | | |
| | | | | |
| | | | | |
| | | | | |
| | | | | |
| | | | | |
| | | | | |
| | | | | |
| | | | | |
| | | | | |
| | | | | |

NOTE:
_____
_____
_____
_____
_____
_____

| Company name: | |
|---|---|
| stock code: | |

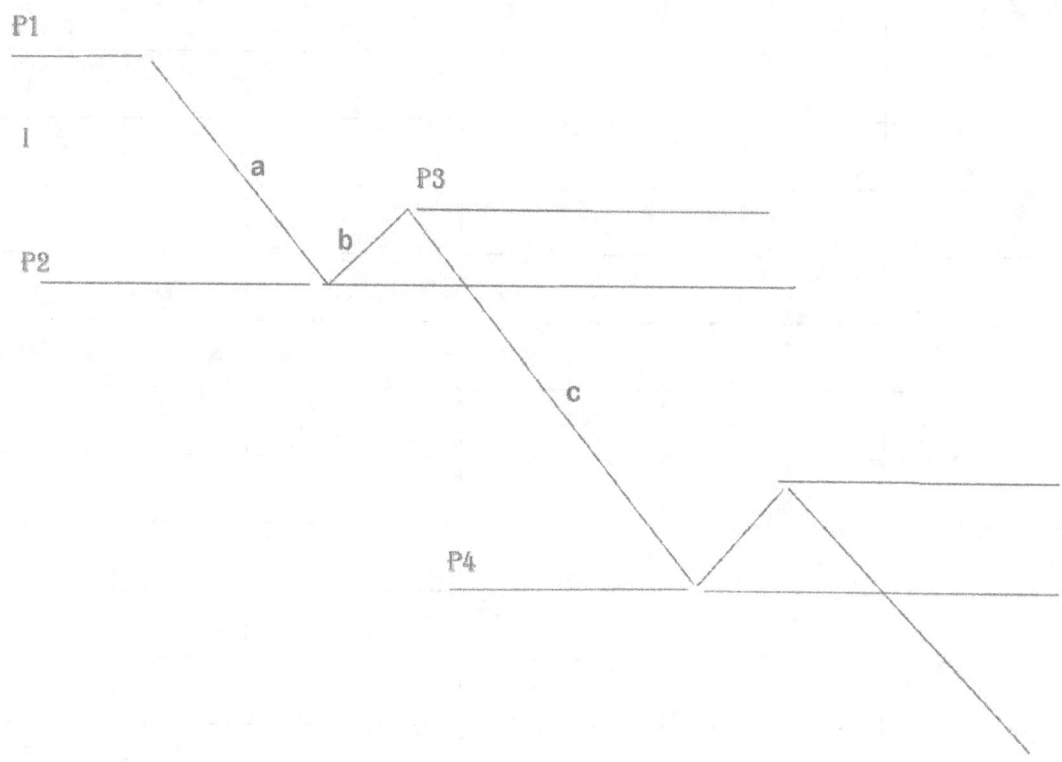

| P4 | I=P1-P2 | |
|---|---|---|
| POSSIBLE | P1-I*1.382= | |
| VALUE | P1-I*1.618= | |

| Risk-reward ratio | Estimated Buying back price | Estimated Overselling price | Acceptable Loss price | Profit (or loss) (according to Risk-reward ratio) |
|---|---|---|---|---|
| | | | | |
| | | | | |
| | | | | |
| | | | | |
| | | | | |
| | | | | |
| | | | | |
| | | | | |
| | | | | |
| | | | | |
| | | | | |
| | | | | |
| | | | | |
| | | | | |
| | | | | |
| | | | | |

NOTE:

| Company name: | |
| stock code: | |

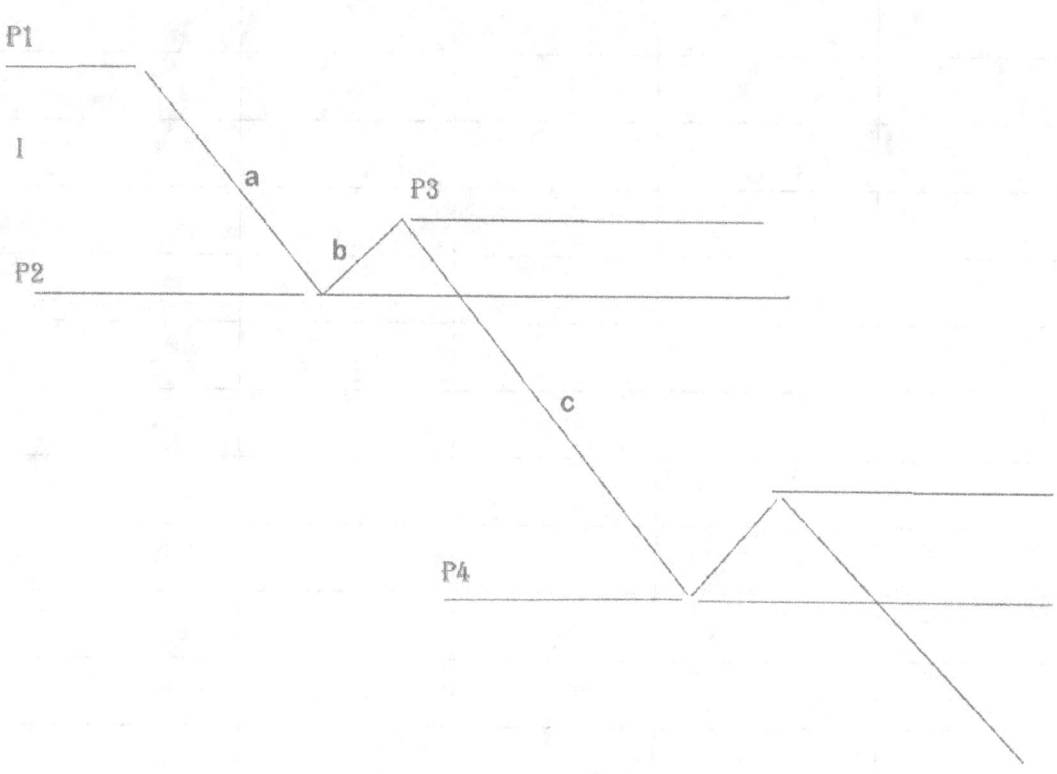

| P4 | I=P1-P2 | |
| --- | --- | --- |
| POSSIBLE | P1-I*1.382= | |
| VALUE | P1-I*1.618= | |

| Risk-reward ratio | Estimated Buying back price | Estimated Overselling price | Acceptable Loss price | Profit (or loss) (according to Risk-reward ratio) |
|---|---|---|---|---|
| | | | | |
| | | | | |
| | | | | |
| | | | | |
| | | | | |
| | | | | |
| | | | | |
| | | | | |
| | | | | |
| | | | | |
| | | | | |
| | | | | |
| | | | | |
| | | | | |
| | | | | |
| | | | | |
| | | | | |

NOTE:

| Company name: | |
|---|---|
| stock code: | |

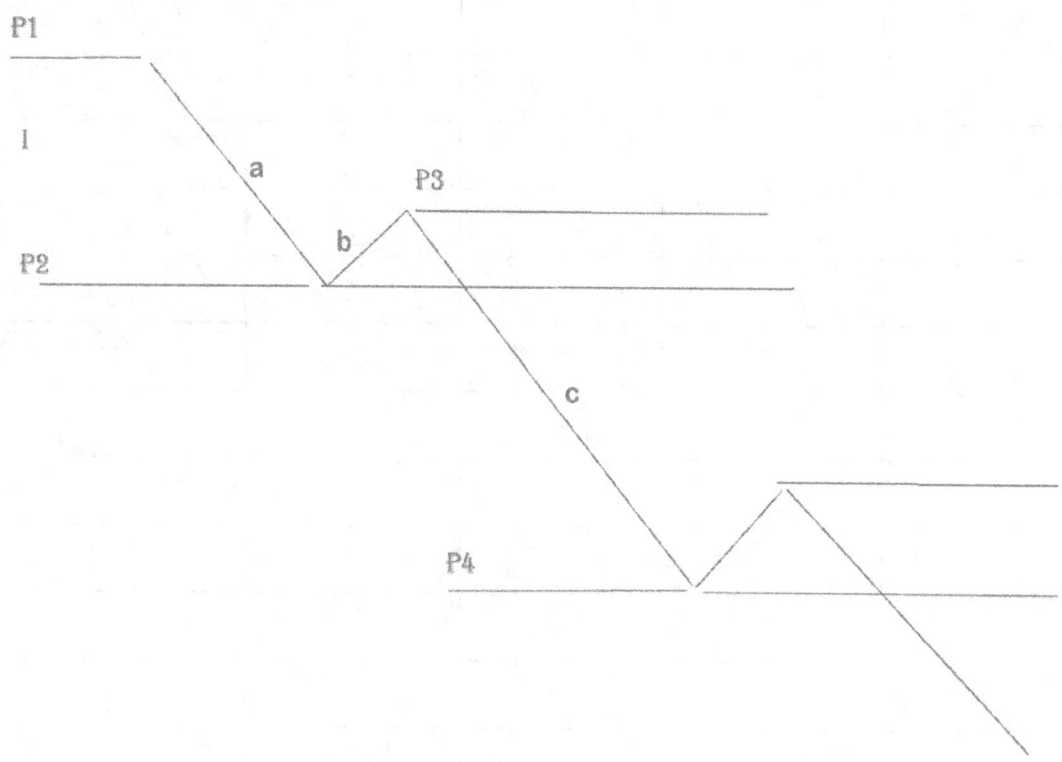

| P4 | I=P1-P2 | |
|---|---|---|
| POSSIBLE | P1-I*1.382= | |
| VALUE | P1-I*1.618= | |

| Risk-reward ratio | Estimated Buying back price | Estimated Overselling price | Acceptable Loss price | Profit (or loss) (according to Risk-reward ratio) |
|---|---|---|---|---|
| | | | | |
| | | | | |
| | | | | |
| | | | | |
| | | | | |
| | | | | |
| | | | | |
| | | | | |
| | | | | |
| | | | | |
| | | | | |
| | | | | |
| | | | | |
| | | | | |
| | | | | |
| | | | | |

NOTE:

www.ingramcontent.com/pod-product-compliance
Lightning Source LLC
Chambersburg PA
CBHW060424220526
45465CB00008B/2999